Praying Clear Through

A book on a subject essential to all who would get into a state of grace, and grow therein; also for those who study to shew themselves approved unto God, workmen that need not to be ashamed.

By

REV. WILLIAM J. HARNEY

Preacher - Evangelist

"O Thou, by whom we come to God,
The Life, the Truth, the Way;
The path of prayer Thyself hast trod:
Lord, teach us how to pray."

GOD'S REVIVALIST PRESS
Cincinnati, Ohio.

AN EARNEST PRAYER

Our Father, assist us as we open this book, to get out of each and every chapter, that Thou hast in each thought, for each and every reader. May we read slowly, cautiously, digesting all we read. Forbid we should be surface readers, but grant us Thy good Spirit to help us to use our picks, drills and sledges, getting down into every thought and out of every thought that which will help us most. Too many read just to be reading. Too few really get into the thoughts. Lead us and may we follow. Help us to study, to be real students. Bless each reader and grant us Thy continued presence. Bless this book. Thou knowest the hours in real soul travail, the tears and heart agony it cost the AUTHOR.

CONTENTS

CONTENTS.

PREFACE

It has been the author's firm conviction that the crying need of this age is a praying Christianity. When the weakest saint falls upon his knees the devil trembles. If the weakest can cause him to fear, what about a Daniel? a Paul? One's experience is as rich and his faith as strong as his prayer life. In all my ministry, we have never failed when we could get the church on her knees. Christians all over the country having read our articles, and heard our sermons and lectures on this vital subject, have begged us for this book. We know that the prayer life is the Christian's force, the Christian's power-house, and the more we pray the stronger will we be against evil and for the right.

We have not written this book for the learned man, nevertheless he can find food for his soul, but for those who want, and need, help in their prayer life. We have written this book while upon the field of battle and in the thickest of the fight, where God answered by fire every heart-cry of His children.

PREFACE.

Let me urge each and every reader to begin to-day a constant waiting upon God; an unrelenting, deep, quiet prayer life. We must get quiet to get the ear of God. We know, by twenty-five years' experience, that God will hear, and that God does answer prayer. We wish for every reader a burden for prayer, a hunger for prayer. We must pray. We must never quit just because we do not get the answer at once. When God leads out in prayer, follow earnestly. He is leading, there is something ahead. Take notice, look, listen, get ready. The cloud is rising. There is soon to be a going in the mulberry-trees. Do not read one chapter and quit the book, but give each and every chapter a faithful reading.

The saint who has done most for God and his fellows has been the one who has prayed most, for it is through this channel that we get the working grace. We will do more, and that the easier, by living upon our faces longer. It is very destructive to rush into the white harvest-fields with a prayerless life. It spells defeat to God. The man who is winning most souls for God is he who lingers much and long in the closet of prayer.

Yours in much prayer,

WILL J. HARNEY.

INTRODUCTION

"Take time to pray!
When fears and foes distress you,
And tiresome toils oppress you,
Then the Master waits to bless you,
If you'll take time to pray.

"Take time to pray!
Come what there may
To stand in the way:
Look often to Jesus
And take time to pray."

"I will therefore that men pray everywhere, lifting up holy hands, without wrath and doubting." (1 Tim. 2:8.) "The effectual fervent prayer of a righteous man availeth much." (Jas. 5:16.) "Let us therefore come boldly unto the throne of grace, that we may obtain mercy, and find grace to help in time of need." (Heb. 4:16.) "When thou prayest, enter into thy closet, and when thou hast shut thy door, pray to thy Father which is in secret; and thy Father which seeth in secret shall reward thee openly." (Matt. 6:6.)

INTRODUCTION.

The author could not have chosen a more important subject on which to write. Indeed, if every Holiness book contained one or more chapters on prayer; or rather, if the opening and closing chapters of every book were on this great theme, it would not be amiss, for to-day there is a universal confession among Christians of "neglect of the secret closet." Jesus said, "Men ought always to pray and not faint," and is not this *neglect* the cause of so many falling away from the Truth, so many not going on unto perfection?

The author caught the vision and has seen the reality of that vision through the secret of Prevailing Prayer. The book is only a record of how God answers him who calls; how God gives victory to the man who *will hear* from Heaven.

We send it forth trusting the Holy Spirit to use it to enlighten the children of God on the attacks of the enemy on the "secret chamber;" to arouse them to the glorious possibilities of prevailing prayer; to help them learn the secret of "Praying Clear Through." Amen!

Read it; study it; obey its injunctions; and for God's glory, circulate it.

MEREDITH G. STANDLEY.

CHAPTER I.

How to Pray Clear Through.

"Ask, and it shall be given you; seek, and ye shall find; knock, and it shall be opened unto you." (Matt. 7: 7.) "If ye shall ask anything in my name, I will do it." (John 14: 14.) "If ye abide in me, and my words abide in you, ye shall ask what ye will, and it shall be done unto you." (John 15: 7.) "And the prayer of faith shall save the sick, and the Lord shall raise him up, and if he have committed sins, they shall be forgiven him." (James 5: 15.) "Elias was a man subject to like passions as we are, and he prayed earnestly that it might not rain, and it rained not on the earth by the space of three years and six months. And he prayed again, and the heaven gave rain, and the earth brought forth her fruit." (James 5: 17, 18.) "And this is the confidence that we have in him, that if we ask anything according to his will, he heareth us.

And if we know that he hear us whatsoever we ask, we know that we have the petitions that we desired of him." (1 John 5: 14, 15.)

For one to pray clear through, necessarily, first, there must be a burden, an object in view; something must have been pressed upon your mind by the Spirit that needs praying for, or about. Here is a child very sick. The doctors tell the parents that the child is most likely going to die. Someway the parents feel led out in prayer for the healing of the child's body. They read some promises, they wait upon God. They pray, and there comes upon them a spirit of prayer, a burden of prayer. There come upon them arguments, poetry, prose, promises, and they really get into soul travail. They fast, they cry to God, they agree, the fire falls, the witness comes. They pray clear through. The child gets well.

One morning while a good woman was washing her dishes, a burden of prayer seized her spirit for a missionary friend in India. She saw that her friend was in great danger, bodily danger, danger of being killed. She saw robbers on her track. She saw them pursuing her. She fled to her bedroom, fell upon her knees, and prayed right through to God, and her friend was gloriously delivered.

One may not get into the spirit of prayer the minute he goes to prayer, or the second he falls upon his knees. It may take quite a little while to get into the spirit of prayer, to get in touch with the forces of the skies. Sometimes when we get up to build a fire there is just a coal or a small chunk of fire. What do we do? We shave some fine kindlings; place them upon the coals of fire; then blow lightly until a small blaze leaps up. Then put on some more kindling; then we put on the fuel, and soon there is a roaring fire, and the room is comfortably warm.

Oftentimes when we've gone to prayer, we were dry, and the devil did his best to keep us dry, but we had gone to prayer, and meant to pray clear through before we quit. We had taken it by the job. We were not in a hurry. We had plenty of time for prayer. We would read the 21st Psalm, the 91st Psalm, the 14th chapter of St. John, 13th chapter of 1st Corinthians, testify to His goodness, meditate, reflect, sing "Jesus Lover of My Soul," pray awhile, praise Him, and keep this up. Don't quit. Don't get up off your knees. Stay down until you hear from Heaven. Stay there until you get into a spirit of prayer. We get what we want, that is, we get what we pray for. If we want the spirit of prayer badly enough, and will go down in earnest, it will be ours to enjoy.

A young man who was convinced that a Methodist pastor should have a helpmeet, began to cast his eyes about, and at last they fell upon a handsome young lady, the sister of a great Congressman. She was well educated, and a great musician. The preacher said, "She just suits me. She can carry on the musical side of the parish, and that is a great help." But he went to prayer. He fasted and prayed. He went daily before God over this all-important step, for much hinges upon this step. He knew that many a preacher's life had been injured, his ministry hurt, by choice of a wrong companion; hence this preacher waited upon God. Seemingly, he could not get into the spirit of prayer. Seemingly, he could not get the ear of God, and he could not get the mind of God. But he kept praying. One time he prayed clear through, and the Spirit said, "No, she's not the woman for you."

Thirteen years had come and gone, and this preacher had become a famous evangelist. Conducting a series of meetings in a large Southern city, he saw an eminent lawyer one night at the altar, crying and pleading with God for pardon. He knelt by the lawyer's side; placing his arms

about him, he said, "Sir, what is your trouble?"
The lawyer looked up into his face, and said,
"May I have a private interview with you to-
morrow?" During the conference the lawyer
said to the preacher, "I married Congressman
So-and-so's sister. She was a beautiful woman,
well educated, and a great musician, but she is
making life a hell on earth to me." When this
preacher got back into his room, he jumped all
over the floor, clapping his hands, and praising
God that he didn't get her for a wife. You see
if the devil could have kept that preacher from
praying clear through, perhaps he would have
gotten that woman, and thousands of souls would
not have been saved.

When a burden comes upon your soul, or the
Spirit leads you out along any line in prayer, take
time, plenty of time to get alone with God in
prayer. Stay there. Don't get up. Don't be
in a hurry. Don't get nervous. Don't look at
your watch. Never stop until you get the mind
of God. It is dangerous to your own soul; it is
destructive to God's cause committed to you. It
will cause you to lose the blessed spirit of prayer,
when He leads you out, and you fail to follow;
fail to stay upon your knees; fail to pray clear
through. God would not burden your heart, God

would not make you hungry, lead you out, causing you to wrestle, to agonize, to fast and pray, unless He meant to answer. It's proof of the fact when the burden continues, and the Spirit continues to lead you out, that there's an answer, and God wants you to pray clear through.

A good woman who was tied to her bed by a malady, prayed three years, once every day, for one hour, for a great revival to break out in her home church, in her home town. Sunday after Sunday she would ask her sister, who was taking care of her, when she came from church, whether anything had happened. Had anything new taken place? God kept burdening her. The spirit of prayer kept leading her out. She became more anxious. She would weep and cry, but every Sunday when her sister came in from church, she told her that the same old, dry folks prayed those long, dry prayers, and the choir sang so but few in the audience could understand anything they said, and the preacher discussed science, and there was nothing being done. The devil teased this honest heart. He said, "You prayed and cried and fasted for three years, and there isn't a single sign of a revival." But one Sunday morning the sister came in and went right to the bed of her sick sister, saying, "A new preacher preached this morning, and I tell you he was a warm member. He woke things up." That night the sister came home about 10:30, and said the altar was crowded, and there were between two hundred and fifty and five hundred souls blessedly saved in that meeting.

Get on two or three good promises. Press down hard on them. Anchor to them. Things will break up. Things will break loose. Things will break over. God hears you, and His thoughts toward you are good. He will answer. Dare to trust Him anywhere. God always hears and answers prayer.

CHAPTER II.

WAITING UPON THE LORD.

"But they that wait upon the Lord shall renew their strength; they shall mount up with wings as eagles; they shall run, and not be weary; and they shall walk, and not faint." (Isa. 40:31.)

"Waiting upon the Lord!" This suggests the beautiful thought of one's having plenty of time, being in no rush or hurry at all. *Waiting* necessitates one's having plenty of time, no other business to attend to, getting alone with God. It takes patience and forbearance to wait upon God; to await His time, His way, His method or plan. To be in a hurry would spoil the grace, the strength, the courage that comes from waiting upon the Lord.

A woman and her two sons, paid her father a visit. They had to get up at two o'clock in the morning and catch an early train in order to

14

make connections at another city, if they would reach her father's home by night that day. She made the first train all right, but when she arrived in the city where she had to make connections for the train that would carry her to her father's, she was compelled to go across the city two miles in a hack to reach the other depot. The hack-team driver was tired, hence she missed her train two minutes. Rushing up to the ticket window, almost out of breath, she asked the agent "if the train going to —— was on time?" He replied, "The train has just pulled out." She wrung her hands and exclaimed, "Oh, isn't that awful! It is simply too bad that I missed that train! That old hack team, those old bony horses did not go fast enough! That driver was a poky man! Tell me, will I have to wait here six hours and a half? Six hours and a half before I can catch a train for my father's!" "Yes, you will have to wait six and a half hours." She went over and took a seat and sat there crying and worrying and be-meaning the hack driver. In about one and a half hours the ticket agent rushed out and across the station to her exclaiming, "Oh, lady, you should rejoice, you should be very happy in miss-ing that train, you saved your life and the life of your two children! That train was derailed and killed the engineer and fireman and flagman and thirteen passengers!" She clapped her hands and cried, "O God, how I thank Thee! I praise Thee for permitting me to miss that train!" How often we misjudge, misunderstand God's providential leadings.

Last December the author took very ill. For ten days and nights we waited much in God's presence, but could not pray through for healing. We cried in earnest, agonizing prayer by the hour, but the clouds were black; His face seemed heavily veiled; there was not one ray of light. The enemy sent us platoons of imps to tease and harass our soul. The devil whispered, "Now you have prayed through before, you have been healed before, what is the matter this time? Why cannot you get a grip upon God now? Why does He not hear your earnest cries?" These suggestions were awful to be whispered into the ear of a trusting soul during such a battle with the enemy, but we remembered that God said, *"They that wait upon the Lord"*—not work, not run, not preach, not sing, but *wait*. It takes more grace to wait than it does to work. It takes more power to tarry than it does to go. Going is easy, going is luxury, but the command is to *wait, wait,* and we must patiently wait, we must wait until we hear from

Heaven, we must wait until we get the mind of God, until we understand His will, His plans, until we know His commands, until He gives us the chart, map and compass.

One day while we were in earnest prayer, our soul in agony, we called upon our good wife to pray. While she was praying most earnestly for us, we looked up into His dear, sweet face with streaming eyes and crushed soul, and begged Him for a promise, begged Him to show us how to go on. The devil had been telling us for several days that we had taken sick to die, that our life's work was ended, that God had no further use for us, that our mission had been fulfilled. Someway, somehow, we could not believe it, and while looking up into His face, begging for light, begging for a promise and asking if it were His will that we should not die in that awful hour, in that dark hour, He gave us this precious promise (St. John 21:23): "Then went this saying abroad among the brethren, that that disciple should not die." We jumped to our feet, clapped our hands, and praised God aloud. Oh, the rushing tides of joy that filled and thrilled and electrified our being! We were carried out into mid ocean upon the billows of His mighty love, but there were lessons to learn, there were experiences to go through,

certain lines of discipline that were essential to
be given us.

Someway, somehow, even though so blessed,
we did not get a grip upon Him for healing, so
went to Christ Hospital in Cincinnati and were
operated on.   The next day after the operation
the devil came in and said, "This is a short route
to the cemetery.   You are going to take blood
poisoning and die."   The nurses would come in
every few moments and take our temperature.
Finally we asked, "What is the matter?   Why
are you taking our temperature so often?"   One
answered, "The doctor fears blood poisoning."
After she had gone out we cried to our God, "Why
did you give us that beautiful promise that
bright promise in St. John 21 : 23, if we are going to die?   Why did you not permit us to die at
home with wife and babies?   Why bring us down
here to this hospital to die among strangers?"
Then our soul stretched out for God and we began to earnestly *wait* upon God.   Suddenly someone whispered, "God can give you another promise; God can give you light; God can show you
that your mission is not accomplished, that your
life work is not ended, that God has need of you
in the great harvest-field."

Just then He gave us this precious promise

(St. John 21:18): "Verily, verily, I say unto
thee, When thou wast young, thou girdest thyself, and walkedst whither thou wouldest: but
when thou shalt be old, thou shalt stretch forth
thy hands, and another shall gird thee, and carry
thee whither thou wouldest not." Here we raised
a shout and praised God that we were to live to
be an old man. You see if we had not *waited*
upon God our soul would have sunk beneath the
waters of discouragement. The devil would have
beclouded our skies, placed a film over our vision,
but we were waiting upon God, we were being
led by the Holy Ghost. Oh, if we would only
wait more upon God! Linger more in His presence! Have more blessed seasons of real, earnest
prayer!

Too often we do not get anywhere in prayer,
we quit before we begin, we get no strength, no
courage, and the prayer life becomes dry and like
stale bread. We do not enjoy it, we do not relish
it, it is a drag, but the deep prayer life is an enjoyable life. It is a life that counts for God and
lifts humanity; it is a life that brings thirty, sixty
and one hundred fold. Men who pray *do* things
for God, they are worth while, they are the men
who bring things to pass.

We cannot accomplish anything for God without this deep prayer life. Waiting upon God in secret prayer prepares one for public proclamation of His truth; prepares one to sing with spirit; prepares one to pray in the Spirit; prepares one to teach under the inspiration of the Spirit. It makes home duties light, it makes work for God a delight, it oils up the machinery. There is no burden, no worry. There is rest, sweet rest, constant rest, abiding rest. No tossing, no sliding, no slipping up, but the abiding peace of God in the heart. Oh, why not *wait* upon God!

CHAPTER III.

Waiting upon God (continued).

This beautiful Scripture discloses the attitude of the soul that grows—waiting before the Lord, for the Spirit to give light, direction. The reason we are so often defeated is because we rush into battle without waiting for His direction.

Waiting means for us never to be in a hurry when we are before the Lord. Waiting means that we have plenty of time, nothing to cause us to get impatient, nothing to worry us. We have all the time needed for this waiting. Patience is a rich grace to manifest in these hours of waiting; in fact, one cannot make progress without it. One cannot wait on God and have his mind wandering. It would kill all the sweet joy that comes to those who do really wait.

You must have concentration, you must get right down before God, and your mind and thought, your *all*, must be there too. You cannot wait on Him with half the heart. He must have all or none. "When thou prayest, enter into thy closet," is His way for us to wait. A whole-hearted service is what pleases Him and puts you in right relationship to get all He can give you in one short life.

Wait, be still, listen, let Him talk, get quiet, close your mouth, you talk too much; give Him a chance to talk to you. He wants to reveal His will to you, His plans for you; His field needs you. He is about to speak, be still, listen to His gentle voice, draw in your mind, prepare the way, He desires a talk with you, get ready. Your mind, soul and body must be prepared for His coming. We can never get His ear until we get quiet before Him. The devil is wise to try to get us all in a hurry, all confused, all nervous, our minds divided, then it is impossible for us to get a grip in prayer. We need plenty of time when we go to pray; more time than anything else; more time than we know what to do with, then we can wait His time and not be in a hurry.

To wait means to get down and stay down, not to get up until you are through, to stay all day, yes, all night, and next day, too, and three whole days and nights, and still longer if necessary. Amen! Glory! It means that you are determined to go through with Him at any cost. It means, too, that you are His to go, or stay, or send. Amen! It means that you are seeking His will to know, His light to follow. It means that you are an honest soul and want light. You are after an open door, and will gladly enter quickly.

Waiting should have your best time, not the close of the day when your mind is tired and sleep has taken hold upon you, but early hours when you are fresh. You should never wait until your mind is crowded with other matters. One will need all his mind to wait on God. Waiting is half the battle. It is that that qualifies us for battle and gives us the assurance beforehand. All the soul-savers get to Him early in the morning. No better time could one find to wait on Him, for His guidance, for the light needed. While others slumber you wait, and you will have the power, and the victory too. Waiting is not easy, but it will pay. Oh, to be still before Him, the whole man patient, just simply waiting God's time! I will stay here until He speaks.

Never come in a hurry, never leave in a hurry, take time to wait, have leisure when you come to wait. Take a vacation. Throw off every care, every burden, all worry. You must wait, your

soul needs this waiting, but it will take time, de-
termination, will power, faith.

CHAPTER IV.

Waiting upon God (concluded).

An earnest, faithful Methodist preacher, while attending a Holiness camp-meeting, had light flashed across his pathway until he saw his privilege in Christ Jesus and rushed into the fountain and was gloriously sanctified. The joy was great, the blessing had burned up the "old man" (we mean that the cleansing had destroyed the "old man"), and there was a haven of rest in his soul. He went home praising God for such a work of grace, but his wife flew into a rage and said, "You have ruined your future and we will starve or be sent to Hard Scrabble Circuit." The faithful man of God flung himself before the Lord in earnest prayer.

Sure enough, they were sent to a poor circuit and things, seemingly, went bad and the clouds were black, not one ray of light. All the flour, all the meat, and in fact everything was at a low ebb.

25

His wife had completely backslidden and was making it very hard for this faithful, sanctified husband. She said to him one night, "If you will get your God to send in one big ham, fifty pounds of flour, three or four dozen eggs, eight or ten pounds of lard, twenty-five pounds of sugar, then I will believe in your holiness. I must see. You are not to speak to a living soul about it. You say that He will answer, now let's see. You can certainly get a prayer through by morning and I can make some good biscuits for breakfast and we will have good, red ham gravy too."

The earnest man of God went to his knees in soul agony. He plead His word. He stepped out on His promises and would never let go until He answered by fire. He got into soul travail about midnight, and about three went to bed knowing that his Lord had heard his heart-cries and would answer. In retiring, he woke his wife, and she said, "Now, good red ham gravy for breakfast?" He said, "Oh, yes, and more too. There will be two hams." "Oh! my dear, do you tell me so?" "Yes," he said firmly. In a few minutes she said, "I do believe that I heard the dogs dragging that ham under the floor." He said, "You rest assured the ham will be here." He fell asleep, but she awoke him saying, "The dogs are fighting over the hams." He quoted some promises, but she laughed heartily. He found out that it was impossible to get any sleep, so he got up and went to earnest prayer. Soon the same gentle witness came whispering, "I have heard your cries, and a surprise awaits your wife." He leaped, he cried, he shouted. His wife came in saying, "The hams must be here the way you are taking on; start me a fire in the stove, it is daylight."

The faithful preacher went at it in a hurry, for he knew his Lord was about ready to start His delivery wagon. While he built the fire, his wife prepared her toilet. Just as the fire was burning well she said, "If you will be so kind as to set that flour and ham on the cook table, I will begin breakfast." Just then a knock at the kitchen door. The preacher opened the door, and there stood a grocer with a ham in one hand and fifty pounds of flour on his shoulder, saying, "I could not sleep at all last night, and something kept saying, 'Take hams and flour to the Methodist preacher's early in the morning.' And there is more coming as soon as my boy gets out the wagon." The preacher turned to his wife and said, "Now!" By that time the wife had fallen full length on the floor, calling to her husband to pray for her, and saying, "Do pray in earnest, or I will soon be in Hell." She confessed and repented and was powerfully saved.

Waiting before Him prepares one to stand still and see the salvation of God. It qualifies us to stand the testings, too. It strengthens our faith. It will rift the clouds and give us a grip on Him that will bring the needed victory. It gives one deep satisfaction. It brings the witness. It puts one in constant telephonic connection with the skies. It makes us more than conquerors, victors on every battlefield.

Waiting before Him gives us the assurance before the battle is fought. This renews us, makes us stronger. There is no need of our depleted condition. There is strength for us and waiting gives it to us. We must wait, or we will lose. Altars should be crowded all the time, and this is all done by much waiting before Him. Hours are needed here, for us to be qualified for the great work He has called us to do.

God needs giants to-day, and we get the giant strength by waiting before Him. Oh, the beautiful soul rest, the strong faith we would have if we would wait on Him.

I have been gloriously healed this year. Doctors said I could never be well again, but I am, and it was done by waiting in earnest prayer. I am a stout man to-day. I weigh 191. I am fat. Amen! I tell you God will hear and answer to-day, and heal too. Glory to His holy name! I am on the mountain. Amen! He is so good to me. Oh, praise His holy name! Dare to trust Him and your case in His hands, and see if He will not answer by fire. Amen! Well, I am having a great time. This is a great summer. Altars are full. Souls are being saved and believers are being sanctified. Let's wait. Get still. Get quiet before Him. Give Him time. Don't be in a hurry. Take time, plenty of time, to wait; more waiting will make your work lighter and you will be rested when the task is done. More waiting will make you better able to do more, and you will have more power to work. First, wait, then work. Wait three hours, and then you will do more in half the time, and be rested, too, when done. Waiting oils the machinery until there isn't a jar or friction. Waiting puts fire in the box, water in the boiler, and steam in the chest, and the old train flies down the track. Waiting draws out the latent facilities, toughens the muscles, and gives one ballast and roadbed. Waiting makes us masters of every situation and so qualifies us that we enjoy doing things for Him.

CHAPTER V.

Silent Times for Prayer.

The prayer life is a sweet, enjoyable life to live, and, in fact, no one can enter into the deep things of God who does not live in a spirit of *constant* prayer. (1 Thess. 5: 17.) One does not have to be upon his knees all the time to do this. A man does not have to lie awake at night, and constantly keep his mind upon that one thing (loving his wife) to see if he really loves her. Awake or asleep, the love is there; at work or pleasure, the love for her burns. Many of God's faithful saints have testified to the fact that often they have wakened up to the fact that tears were flowing, joys leaping, fire burning, and that, too, while they were busy.

Excuse the writer for a personal reference. Once, while plowing corn, old Jack, a faithful mule, was pulling the plow, his long ears keeping time with his feet. No one was near; corn almost over Jack's back; we were in a spirit of prayer. All at once the tide came in, and Jack went through that corn in a hurry.

"Rejoice evermore" does not mean one must shout all the time at the top of the voice; it means to live in the spirit of rejoicing. So it is with the prayer life, to live in the spirit of prayer. But mind you, there will be times of waiting upon your knees by the hour. There will be seasons of wrestling prayer. There will be protracted seasons of prayer.

The prayer life calls for seasons of silent times, times when we take ourselves away from the crowd, family, loved ones, business, and get quiet before Him. One can be too busy about his Master's work and neglect these quiet, silent times, and become lean, grow peevish, fretful, cross. Too often we talk too much when we pray. We do not give God a chance to say one word, and not a few times, we do nothing but beg—beg—beg; there is no note of praise or thankfulness.

There was one college that had, every morning and evening, a silent time; no sound was heard —no lessons studied—all was silent. The whole college was as quiet as if all had been in slumber. One could feel the Spirit of prayer all about the college.

If every one who professes to be His would have one-half hour daily, in quiet prayer, the great revival would rush upon us.

We mean by quiet times, getting off alone, going into one's closet, getting away from all business, getting all out of one's mind—*getting alone with GOD*.

The crying need of the day is earnest prayer, wrestling prayer, a praying that brings things to pass. Paul and Silas brought things to pass at Philippi.

This is a busy age, all hands are full from daylight until dark. One said, "I can't take from my business thirty minutes each day." A preacher said to the writer, "I can't find time to pray, I pray on the run all the time." One may be in the spirit of prayer on the run, but there must come into every Christian's life silent times, if we are to be worth while.

Look at those whom God is using to-day. Stanley Jones of India, a young man who lives upon his knees. Bud Robinson, a man who really brings things to pass, upon his knees. Look at Jim Upchurch, a walking illustration of what can be done through prayer. I tell you, reader, we must live upon our faces more and talk less, if the great revivals are to come.

The devil hates these quiet, silent times, this living upon your face, for when the weakest saint gets upon his or her knees, he knows it is time for him to tremble.   What does he do when a Paul or Silas gets upon his knees!

You can organize Bible classes, men's movements, laymen's movements, young people's societies (and they all have their places for good), but until there is really knee work, it all will finally run dry.   Prayer oils up the machinery.

One of the greatest needs of this hour is more devotion.   Ours is not an age of prayer so much as an age of work.   The tendency is to action rather than to worship; to busy toil rather than to quiet sitting at the Savior's feet.   Commune with Him.   The key-note of our present Christian life is consecration, which is understood to mean devotion to active service.   On every hand we are incited to work; our zeal is stirred by every inspiring incentive.   The calls to duty come to us from a thousand earnest voices.   And this is well; we must toil in His vineyard, we are His harvest men; we are toilers together with Him. But these quiet, silent times alone qualify us to do more and better work, with much more ease and enjoyment, and nothing slavish about it.

CHAPTER VI.

In the Closet.

In this electric age, most every one is on the run, hands full, head full; on the hurried march from early dawn until late at night answering the many, many calls. One cannot see much time to go to the closet; one can hardly get his eyes open before duty calls strong and loud, and off we hurry to office, business, school, store, shop, without any quiet time before Him. The devil hates prayer, he is aware of the fact that the prayer life is the successful life, hence, he must interrupt some way and if he can get us in a nervous hurry, we will neglect our quiet times and become weaklings and easy to overcome.

In these sad days when all kinds of deviltry are sweeping our land, souls by the tens of thousands being hurried over the Niagara of destruction, it is high time that the watchman upon the walls sound the trumpet loud, calling the children of God to earnest prayer. The soul will grow more in one day in quiet waiting before Him than in a dozen without the quiet time. We cannot *work* our way into His kingdom, we can not *rejoice* our way in. He has said, "Ask, and ye shall receive," and the soul which has quiet times will do more in a revival than two dozen who work, work, work, but nothing more. One can work without religion, but he who lingers, waits, gets still, lets the Holy Ghost reveal His secrets, gets anointed and oiled up, will work and there will be less friction, better service, and more fruit. Watch him who goes aside, as did Moses, from the busy cares and toils of daily life, and you will see him fired and sent forth to lead lost men to God.

More prayer, earnest praying, as did Elijah until the cloud was plainly seen; a wrestling all night, as did Jacob, would usher in upon the Church a great revival, sweet peace, deep peace, a continual flow of rich peace. The joy that abides comes when you get quiet before God daily.

A servant dressing one of God's faithful servants, found corns upon the aged man's knees. Asking why, the old soldier, with eyes full of tears, said, "I have waited so much in my closet, had such blessed quiet times in secret devotion,

that living mostly upon my knees brought corns."
If we had corns upon our knees, no doubt our
work would bear more fruit, but few to-day have
corns upon their knees.

A young Asbury student went out to preach
over the Sabbath. Joe saw the young preacher
go off ever and anon to the barn. He wondered, he
followed, and he found this earnest young man
upon his knees. Slipping back to the house, he
said, "Wife, that young man is religious. In place
of joking, he is off crying for a message and a
work of salvation." Joe said to the writer, "No
one can ever tell how that impressed me, how it
put me into the prayer life, how it taught me the
importance of prayer, how it did impress prayer
upon me." Joe said that a red-hot sermon and
salvation were the results of that secret devotion
in the barn.

Going off alone with God, getting quiet, waiting, not being in a hurry, taking time to pray, will
prepare for public service. It is disheartening to
preach from Sunday to Sunday, and have no one
getting saved, no one at the altar, no one asking
for prayers, and it tends to lessen the possibility
of these things, as it will discourage those who
believe and those who might seek. Why is there
not more urging souls to seek Jesus in every ser-

mon? Because the fire of prayer has died and the service drifts into formality.

A preacher once said, "I shall locate and go into other business, no one cries, laughs, seeks God or joins the church under my ministry." The whole trouble was, briars had grown up in his closet. He was by far too busy to wait before Him. Education, set afire by the Holy Ghost, and a quiet time daily before Him, would bring things to pass for God. Once, after a great sermon, one said, "Was that not about the finest sermon you ever heard?" Another said, "My! he's smart." Another said, "Oh, his head is full of brains." "Yes," said an old saint, "but there is the lack of prayer in his life; such a sermon, coming from a man who had just come from his closet, would have borne some fruit." There was not a tear, a laugh a shout, no one got hungry for Jesus. They went away bragging on the man, not Jesus.

Waiting before God gives courage, makes one bold. No matter who is in the pew, you have a message from the skies. Kill or cure, you are God's man, no bits on you. No rich man's money will quiet your convictions; you do not belong to any clan or clique, but are a servant of the most high God.

A learned doctor had preached a helpful ser-

mon; twenty-two fell at the altar. The workers
had instructed, sung, prayed and were about to
close, when an unpretentious, illiterate country
woman, with her sunbonnet on and a baby astride
her hip, walked down the aisle to the mourners.
She went to one and then another, saying, "Look
up, look to Jesus. He saved me and He will save
you. Believe it, repent, look up." Her face shone
and tears were flowing from her eyes. A number
of seekers leaped up and stood with shining faces,
telling the sweet story. The reason? This country woman lived a part of each day in her closet,
and God rewarded her openly.

It is the prayer life that *counts*. Now get
quiet, quit being in a hurry, take plenty of time to
pray. Luther, when he had an extra heavy day's
work before him, first prayed three hours. Prayer
gives strength, nerve, vitality, and courage;
makes work easy, and the hardest task enjoyable;
it illuminates the darkest corner, and service becomes a real pleasure, having lost all its irksome-
ness. The prayer-meetings and class-meetings
become flower gardens to one's soul. When one
gets into this blessed habit, it is hard to get away
from the closet; one has to fairly pull himself up
off his knees.

You may at first find it hard to keep on your

knees, you may for a few times find your mind away at work, but just be patient, take yourself back. Be determined to conquer and have the victory; enter into your closet, stay there, and soon hours will be enjoyed in this blessed way. Do not give up, do not quit just because God does not answer at once. Never be contentious about anything, but go to your closet the more often, take more time to pray. Never be in a hurry when you pray. Get everything out of your mind; be at leisure; have nothing else to do, and God will bless, for He says, "They that wait upon me shall renew their strength."

CHAPTER VII.

He That Believeth.

"He that believeth on the Son hath the wit-ness in himself." (1 John 5: 10.)

Here we see that we first believe, and by so doing receive the witness. Then why should we seek after the witness? Why not just believe God? As He has said, "By faith ye are saved," the Blood washes sins away for the one who believes. You never can feel, you never can see, you never can know, you never will have the witness, until you *fully believe.* We are saved by faith, we are not saved by the witness, neither are we saved by knowledge. Knowledge comes through faith; the witness comes by faith. Faith is the key that unlocks the great treasure-house and gives us access to all that God has in store for us.

Certainly God would not thrust His children

out upon the great rugged sea of life without chart, map or compass. You will know when you are saved, but mark it! you will first believe. "Because he *trusted* in Thee," not because he *felt* in Thee, not because he *saw* in Thee, but because he *believed*. "Faith is the substance of things hoped for, the evidence of things not seen."

Will you know when you believe? John says, "He that believeth on the Son of God hath the witness."

I went to see an intelligent young lady who was about ready to sail as a missionary. She looked up out of her streaming eyes, and said to me, "Oh, why can I not get the witness? I do not want to be deceived; I do not want to be mistaken; I want to *know* it." We opened the Bible where we had 1 John 5 : 10 fenced in with red ink and pointed our index finger at the verse and she read, "He that *believeth*—" We stopped her and said, "You must not read it that way; read it, 'He that *feeleth*.'" She said, "Mr. Harney, the Bible says, 'He that believeth.'" We said to her, "Are you not seeking knowledge, feelings?" She saw the point, jumped to her feet, ran back into the church, throwing her arms around her father, shouting, "I have the blessing!" How did she receive the blessing? By faith, and that is the

only way one can get it, for that is God's way, and
"he that climbeth up some other way is a thief and
a robber."

Joshua had to shout before the walls fell; at
the Jordan Israel had to step in before the waters
opened up.   Why?   Israel had been brought out
of Egypt through the Red Sea and had been taken
care of by the Lord.   They were His and His
must *believe* without any signs.

A young man came to the altar one night in a
Southern camp-meeting and said, "Brother Harney, tell me how to get saved.   I have been both-
ered for years."   We told him, we read the parts
of the Bible to him that clearly point out the way.
He arose, seemingly without any emotion, and
turning to the congregation, said, "I am saved."
A good old local preacher came up to him, saying,
"You are mistaken; you are deceived.   You can
not be saved, for when I got saved I shouted all
over the camp-ground, and you have not shouted
one bit."   The young man said, "I have done
what God has shown me to do, and I am *believing*
that He saves me just now."   The local preacher's wife said, on their way home, "Young man, I
feel badly for you, and I felt badly for you to-
night, for I am persuaded that you are hood-
winked, misled.   When I got saved I shouted for

about two or three hours." The next morning the old local preacher met the young man at the post-office and said, "How are you feeling by this time?" The young man answered, "I am believing still that God saves me *now.* I have done all He has shown me to do. What else could I do but trust Jesus Christ, and I purpose to do that." The good old local preacher said, "You are mistaken. I tell you when you get salvation you will shout." That night when he came into the tabernacle the local preacher's wife met him and said, "Have you not got the witness yet? Do you not feel that you are saved?" He looked calmly into her face and said, "I believe that God saves me now. There has been no great emotion, no great joy, but I am simply trusting God. As I have said to you before, I repeat, I have done all the Holy Ghost has shown me, and if He shows me anything else I will gladly do it."

The third night, just before we preached, the Spirit led us to sing, "I can, I will, I do *believe.*" We said, "Let us give God a wave offering." All pulled out their handkerchiefs and stood on their feet, and we waved and sang repeatedly, "*I can, I will, I do believe.*" All at once this young man jumped up on top of his seat, waving his handkerchief and shouted, "I am saved, glory to God!"

He came jumping down the aisle shouting aloud, "Jesus saves me!" He was saved by faith. The shouting was only the outward manifestation of the inner joy.

Is not that what God says? Did not God say we are saved *by faith* through grace? When we believe, we are saved. You cannot receive the witness until after you have believed. You must first believe, for we are saved *by faith* through grace. When we believe, great peace flows into our heart. A stability of character takes hold upon us and we are anchored in the haven of rest.

OUR PRAYER.

O Lord, for Jesus' sake, for our sake, for Thy Word's sake, for the Spirit's sake, who gives us light, help Thou us to believe! Help Thou us to trust Thee! May we not waver as the waves of the sea. Keep Thou us from being unsteady and unstable, root us and ground us, give us anchorage, assist us, that our faith in Thee may bring us through to Thy glory and honor. Forbid we should doubt Thee! Oh, may we, Thy children, not dishonor Thee by doubting, but may we step out upon Thy promises, knowing that Thou carest for us! Hear us and give unto us an increase of faith.

CHAPTER VIII.

PLACING OUR FACE BETWEEN OUR KNEES.

"So Ahab went up to eat and to drink. And Elijah went up to the top of Carmel; and he cast himself down upon the earth, and put his face between his knees." (1 Kings 18: 42.)

The incidents that cluster about this rich text of Scripture point out clearly that God sent the needed rain, the long looked-for rain, prayed-for rain, through this man Elijah *placing his face between his knees.* This was the gate which stood ajar for the loving Father to send the gracious rain upon the parched, dry country, thereby clothing the forest in variegated foliage, spreading a carpet of green over the cooked earth, causing the beautiful flowers to spring up, lading the air with fragrant odors, while the song birds, filling the forests with their glad notes, made glad the heart of man and beast. The Lord Jehovah had been waiting for a channel through which to send this glad, good news, but He needed a clean channel, a consecrated channel.

There is nothing that can fail if God sees it is best, that it is for His glory and the salvation of man. Our prayers do not change the plans and purposes of God; they influence the actions of God, not His purposes. It is the devil's business to becloud our spiritual skies, and discourage us. Discouragement is one of the greatest barriers in the Christian's pathway. No man ever had a better cause to become discouraged than did Elijah, and he would have been discouraged had he failed to remember that God and he were a majority. God can undo anything the devil has ever done. The devil fills a man full of sin, full of doubt, full of uncontrollable appetites, but if that man will come to Jesus, *He* will destroy all sin, and the sinner, saved by grace, will stand in His great presence as if he had never transgressed His law. When God forgives a man. He forgets all about his sins, remembers them against him no more.

It is one of the tactics of the enemy to becloud, befog—question the faithfulness of God, and thus a discouraged man can be defeated. He cannot fight, his fighting blood has been frozen, through the devil's channel, discouragement. The Russians went into every battle discouraged, the Japanese went into battle thrilling with courage; hence the Russians were defeated. When we become discouraged, we dishonor God; we help turn the tide in Satan's favor, we assist in defeating God's plans and purposes. It takes a holy man to surmount and conquer discouragement. It takes a holy man to go right ahead when all looks blue —no clouds, no sign of rain. It takes a holy man to live *right* in the midst of discouraging circumstances and keep his heart above the clouds, in the golden sunlight of time. God loves such men, honors such men, uses such men! Holy men are worth while in every walk of life. They are salt to preserve, light to illuminate.

Men love men of stability, of cheerfulness. It is our choice whether we will live on the sunny side of the street, scattering sunshine, or live in the cold, damp shadows, scattering doubts, chilling the faith of His dear saints, placing mountains in the weaker brother's pathway. We can be strong in God, able to do a full day's work, a long day's work, a hard day's work, and not complain, or we can be weak, not fit for anything. A strong man talks strongly, walks with a firm gait, breathes deeply, has a good appetite, enjoys his meals, eats what is placed before him. He is like a signboard, pointing out clearly what good things God can do for those who are strong in Him.

How are we to be kept from discouragement? The first thing is to be certain that we are right with God, that we are regenerated, born of the Spirit, begotten of God, brought from darkness to light, *know* we are His children. Paul says, "We *know* that if this earthly house were destroyed, we have a tabernacle not made with hands, eternal in the heavens." John says, "We *know* because we love the brethren." God is no respecter of persons, and if Paul and John knew, we may also know. We *know* whom we have believed, and are fully persuaded that He is able to keep that which we have committed unto Him against that day.

The second thing is to obey. Walk in all the light God gives, and then when you have done fully your part, wait with patience for Him to do His. Never become discouraged, always remember that the world was not made the first day. When the day's work is done, if we did all that was shown us, if we did our best, if we walked in all the light God gave, even though our work be awkwardly done, if it was our best, He will love us good because we did it to please and honor Him.

One hot summer day I came in from hoeing in the garden, and said to my sweet, black-eyed Helen, but five summers, "Please bring me a glass of water." She hurried off to the kitchen and came back with a glass brimful of water, struck her little foot against a brick and down went baby Helen, water and all. She jumped up, grabbed the glass, looked at me somewhat embarrassed and said, "Wait, father, I will bring you a drink of water." Here she came a second time with a glassful and four little fingers inside of the glass of water, and four streams running down the outside of the glass. I picked up the baby, pressed her tenderly to my heart, and drank the water. She did my errand awkwardly, but she did her best. She knew father loved her and because she did her best, he petted her, and hugged her. We may make mistakes and blunder about, but if we do our best, God will love us and bless us good.

When things do not go our way, we must not give up, but keep right on for God. If work, committed to us does not prosper as we planned and looked for, we are to go right on as if it had prospered. How are we to conquer?—by *placing our face between our knees;* by protracted seasons of fasting and prayer. No one can live without passing through some trials, but we should always remember that the sun can shine behind the clouds, that just beyond the tunnel we will run into the golden sunlight, and by having gone through the tunnel we will appreciate and enjoy the light the more. Yes, discouraging circumstances may surround us, but we may surmount them if we will. We may live such a prayer life that we can extract courage and blessing out of everything that comes to us.

CHAPTER IX.

Ask!

"He placed his face between his knees." (1 Kings 18:42.)

The Master in this Scripture discloses the fact that Elijah is tremendously burdened; God has rolled a crushing burden upon the prophet's heart; he sees, he knows, he understands full well the needs of the people and country. His eyes are open to this, and God purposes through him to send the needed rain. But this man of God must have heart agony, soul travail, before God can send the gracious rain upon the earth and slake the thirst of man and beast. No revival ever has come to any community or church; no soul has ever been saved or sanctified; nobody has ever been healed, but that some soul had real, vital soul travail for that blessing.

God has said Zion must travail as a woman in

childbirth. The church that does not have soul travail cannot have sin-killing, soul-saving revivals. There is no man who has seen his wife travail in childbirth but understands this illustration. God, seemingly, looked all over the world and searched Heaven for a single illustration by which to illustrate the truth, the fact, the importance, of a soul being brought from nature's night into the glorious Gospel light of salvation, and He found but one, and that was, as the woman travails in childbirth, so must the Church.

Some of us have stood by the bedside with surgeons and nurse and watched our precious wives go right down into the jaws of death, into the deep valley of agony—such pains, such suffering, no one understands but those who have had an actual experience. The wife grasped the husband by the hand and cried out, "Can I stand another three minutes like that! I do not believe I can. I thought I was dying." The doctor comes up and encourages; the nurse brushes back the locks, and mops the beads of sweat from the brow. Then another paroxysm of pain—oh, what suffering, what crushing pains, the groans of the wife, the gritting of her teeth, her eyes as it were set in her head, her finger-nails well nigh buried in the flesh. She cries out, "O God! how much longer can I stand this awful suffering?" It is not long until there is a cry; baby has been born.

So the Church must go down into the Garden of Gethsemane. The Christian must get in the valley of agony until there comes into one's soul inwrought prayer, a real crushing burden upon the heart, or we will never pray clear through. We must wake up to the importance, the crying need, and then keep at it, keep at it, keep at it; never let go, never let up; tug away; stand on His promises; cry aloud and spare not. Tell the devil of Discouragement to be gone; command Doubts and Fears to skulk off; look up into God's face, plead His promises, stand upon His immutable Word; cry out, "O God! Thou hast placed this crushing burden upon my heart; something must be done; something must come to pass; my soul is bleeding." Keep at it; do not quit, for oftentimes it will take some time to get down in straight, earnest, heart-wrestling prayer; so keep at it; do not get discouraged; never grow faint-hearted. If the answer is delayed, keep at it the more; keep at it the harder; go after it the stronger; be more determined than ever; keep at it, for as long as your heart is burdened and the Holy Ghost leads you, the answer is certain to come—keep at it!

Elijah covered up his lookers. He would not,

he could not, afford to look. It is never by sight, but always by faith, for "we are saved by faith, through grace, and that not of ourselves, it is the gift of God." Prayer is the key that unlocks the barn door, and faith, the horse, gallops off through the meadowland.

The crying need of this age is a crushing burden of prayer. The original word for soul travail, heart agony, is illustrated by the soldier life. The soldier toils; he must be disciplined; the burning sun boils upon him, the roads are dusty, but he must be disciplined. He does not drill one day, one week, one month, and stop, but he keeps at it. He must obey the captain, the general; his life is one of toil and labor. He drills, drills, drills; cold or hot, summer or winter, year in and year out, he keeps at it. That is the way he reaches the goal.

The original of this figure discloses that one must wrestle in prayer as a friend strives to save a friend from a watery grave. How quickly, how anxiously, we throw ourselves into the water and swim out, risking our own lives, to drag our friend from a watery grave.

One great trouble is that we simply repeat words, phrases, and sentences; the heart must get into it. One of God's saints prayed until he had nose bleed; another prayed until he vomited; another until the blood burst from the pores of the skin. Think of such agony!

We should give God the early hours of the morning, when the mind and body are rested, and we are fresh and vigorous. No wonder the churches are losing their attraction and are largely empty, and have resorted to questionable means and practices to raise finances. No wonder preachers are leaving the pulpit and saying their ministry is barren, and the pews are empty. It is all because there is a lack of earnest, protracted heart agony in prayer. Look at the "Mount of Blessings." There the fire is always falling; souls are continually being saved, believers plunging into the fountain, the sick being healed, and missionaries going forth to tread the dark continents of earth—and all this because of *prayer*.

When a church lives upon its knees, her pews are full, her coffers run over, and there are no kitchen department, no bazaar, no broomdrills, no auctions, no gambling, no suppers needed. When a preacher has calloused knees, cries by the hour over his message and people, sees keenly the needs of his people, *prays clear through*, souls are at the altar finding God, and he brings forth more fruit. His face is aglow, and the joybells ringing; deep down in his soul is an artesian well, and the rich fruits of Canaan are loading his table.

Elijah had the burden; he knew God had placed it upon his heart; hence he must pray clear through—get the victory—or lose his grip. When God places a burden upon one's heart there is a crying necessity, there is a demand, and we as channels must let this blessing come through us to the needy ones. An illustration of this. An honest country mother, who was saved and blessedly sanctified and walked close to God, and who lived much upon her knees, had real, sweet, blessed communion with the Father, Son and Holy Ghost, understood the language of prayer, and had been taught how to linger upon her knees, sat in my audience one night as I preached a sermon on "The Prodigal Son." A burden came upon her heart for the salvation of her drummer boy. She did not know where he was, had not heard from him for some time, but the burden slipped into her soul while we were preaching. The tears flowed from her eyes. She went home, but could not rest. No sleep, the burden was pressing, growing heavier; something must be done. She could not stand it, so she called her niece. Taking her own lamp, she walked back to the church (a half mile distant), unlocked the church doors, and she and her niece entered God's sanctuary near midnight. She read His promises; she got down at the altar upon her face; she cried; she moaned; she groaned. The burden was awful; her soul was in agony. She knew something was coming. That boy had been placed upon her heart at this time as never before. Her soul was troubled. She cried out, "My God! My God!" Hear this broken-hearted mother's prayer. "Send the Holy Ghost to my boy just now. Wake him up. Alarm him. Stir him. Show him his lost and undone condition." Two o'clock came, and yet but very little light. She kept at it. She was a wheel horse. She knew all would be lost if she were to let up or let go; no distraction, nothing must call her off of the wires; she must *pray through*. Three o'clock came. It grew darker, for the darkest hour is just before day. Seemingly, demons thick and fast gathered about that altar. She raised her face and eyes and hands, crying, "My God! My God! forsake me not. Why is it so dark? Thou knowest this crushing burden. Why did it come? Do not let the enemy defeat my soul. Hear me for Jesus' sake, for my broken heart's sake, for my poor troubled soul's sake." Four o'clock came. It had grown darker; fierce gales were coming; thunders were pealing; lightnings were flashing; the little bark was tempest-tossed by the angry waves, but she held on to the oars. Five o'clock came. The awful typhoon had grown to a frightful pitch, but she stuck to her oars, she kept at it, nothing could daunt her. The devils out of Hell and demons on earth could not deter, could not dismay; she said, "I'll die or have the victory." Five-thirty came. The clouds rifted; the sun came up over the eastern horizon; the blessed Holy Ghost took this broken-hearted, weeping, earnest, honest, sincere mother, who had wrestled, who had had real, vital heart agony, who prayed clear through, in His arms, and said, "Your boy is coming home to-morrow, and will get saved."

I had just gotten up, prepared my toilet, and come out on the front gallery, admiring her flower gardens, when she came around the road, waving her bonnet over her head, shouting, crying, laughing, hollowing, "Isn't it wonderful, wonderful, wonderful! God has told my soul—I know it; the Holy Ghost spoke it; I have the burning witness, the blessed, sweet assurance—my drummer boy is coming." Her daughters ran out into the yard and threw their arms about their mother, and here came the sanctified father, and what a time we had in that yard that bright morning! What victory that mother had! She was more than conqueror, her face fairly shone. Eat breakfast? No—she was supping with Him.

That morning at ten o'clock, while I was preaching, in walked a tall, nicely dressed young man. The good old mother (who always sat in a split-bottomed chair in the "Amen Corner") looked up and saw her drummer boy coming down the aisle. She jumped from that chair, and what shouting! She ran to that boy, threw her arms around him, and here they came to the altar in a long trot. That young man was gloriously saved that morning. I said, "How came you here? What brought you here? How were you impressed to get here?" He said, "Brother Harney, last night about midnight, I had a nightmare, or rather, a peculiar force got hold of me, a power got inside of me. Something said, 'Go home at once,' and I was fearful that mother was sick. I never dreamed of going to the altar, but when I opened the church door and saw the church filled with people, and saw the shining face of my sweet mother, an awful conviction leaped into my soul, and I was willing, yea, more than willing, to go to the altar or do anything to get relief—to get saved." He said to me, "It was about twelve o'clock when the alarm bells were turned into my soul." Remember, reader, this was the exact time that that saintly, godly mother had gone down in His house upon her knees for her boy.

God has said, "I will hear when you pray. Ask, and ye shall receive. Ask largely, that your joy may be full." Had this mother listened to the voice of the enemy, looked at the discouragements, she would have given up; she would have gone from that church a defeated woman, and doubtless her boy would have gone to Hell. God put that burden upon her. God knew that was the time for that drummer to get saved, and God also knew that was the time for that mother to wrestle, have heart agony, pray clear through for that boy. That mother was determined: her face was set, and she got the victory for which she prayed.

CHAPTER X.

Not Looking, but Trusting.

1 Kings 18: 42.

There never has been in the history of the world a greater crisis than at this time. The devil had made inroads on God's people; they had backslidden and gone into frightful sins; they had lost connection; their grip upon God had been loosened, and God had to chasten them to win them back, to get their ear, to open their eyes, to wake them up.

God does not delight in afflictions, but if that is the only channel through which He can reach the soul, He will use the rod and spoil not the child. Too often we are so immersed in business, engaged in our pursuits, lost in our callings, that we neglect the all-important thing, waiting, waiting, waiting upon God, in protracted seasons of earnest prayer. We may be engaged in His work.

but, nevertheless, we owe it to ourselves, to our
fellows, and to our God, to have seasons of waiting, patient, heart-searching waiting before Him.

The disciples were blessed in the Upper Room
in a ten-days prayer-meeting, and when they came
from the prayer-meeting they were so qualified
that, in one short service, three thousand were
saved and added to the Church. We are the
weaker when we neglect these protracted seasons
of prayer. We are the less liable to be on the victory side, and more liable to be in the dumps. To
neglect prayer is to neglect feeding the soul, hence
we are too weak to resist the devil and abstain
from all sights of evil. Prayer is God's way, His
peculiar way, one of His essential ways, of feeding the soul. The man that prays much has much
joy and soul rest; he is empowered for service;
his praying, his singing, his preaching, his working—all bear fruit, because He has waited upon
God, and, "They that wait upon the Lord shall
renew their strength; they shall mount up with
wings as eagles; they shall run, and not be weary;
and they shall walk, and not faint."

Elijah "put his face between his knees." He
covered up his eyes—he would not look. Oftentimes to look is to fail. Adam and Eve looked at
the forbidden fruit, fell into sin, and entailed the

awful curse upon poor humanity. Listen to the sighs, sobs, and heart agony! Look at the tears! Think of the deception! Look longer, tens of thousands of mothers' precious daughters housed in slumdom, thrust behind iron bars of lust, tied down to prostituted passion! Look at that mighty army driven by the lash of King Alcohol; see the gallows and the electric chair—and then remember that nine-tenths of the crime is chargeable to King Alcohol —and then you have a faint picture of what was brought upon humanity by that look, by that gaze, of Adam and Eve.

Samson, the mightiest man, the strongest man, one of the most fruitful preachers God ever pitted against Hell's artillery, lost his locks and committed suicide—all because he gazed at Delilah. David, the sweet singer of Israel, the author of the Psalms, who could touch the key-board and the sweet strains of music would chase the wicked spirits away from the first king of Israel, he, even he, lost his hold upon God, hung his harp upon a willow, and was thrust into the deep dungeon of apostasy, by gazing through a window at Mrs. Uriah. Judas lost his house and lot in Heaven by gazing at the bag of money. Joshua commanded the people to stone Achan to death because of his hellish gaze at the shekels of silver, the Babylonish garment, and golden wedge.

Elijah would not, and could not afford to, look at surroundings and circumstances; to look would have meant discouragement; to look would have defeated God's purpose; to look would have forever locked up the clouds and kept back the rain; to look meant he would never have been the channel through which God sent the gracious rain; to look would have lost all. So he covered up his lookers, just would not look.

It is not by sight, but by faith, that the victory is won, and faith has no lookers; that is, faith does not look at earth, and earthly environments, but faith looks, gazes, upon the Son of God. Illustration: A young lady, a very delicate woman—looked as if she were about eaten up with tuberculosis—in the midst of a gracious revival, arose from the organ stool one night when we were about to dismiss the audience, saying, "Brother Harney, may I just say a few words?" We knew her to be a level-headed, sane young lady, one who did not go at things spasmodically, hence we granted her request. The tears were raining down her face; all could see that she was under a tremendous strain. She said: "Friends and neighbors and kinsmen, you have known me for twenty-seven years; I have taught your town school for seven years; I have been your organist for twelve years; but, I am frank to say that I never have been so burdened in all my life. There is a burden upon my soul that is crushing the very life out of me. I have gladly watched, joyfully watched, these stalwart men rush to the altar and get saved; I have listened to their bright testimonies, and looked into their shining faces with a glad heart. I am rejoicing because God has answered mothers' prayers and saved their sons. The thought just struck me—Why should not my poor drunken brother get to God in this meeting? —and with the thought came this crushing burden, so I want to ask, I want to ask all of you Christians with our good pastor and the evangelist, to cry to God mightily in behalf of my poor drunken brother. I mean to fast. I shall not eat nor sleep nor rest until my drunken brother is sweetly saved."

As she sank in her chair we looked at that tall woman, we looked into her pale face, and as she buried her face in her hands and sobbed aloud, that great audience was moved. Men, stout men, sinners, wept. Her father, an eminent lawyer, jumped to his feet, saying, "Daughter, you must retract, recall that rash vow. You are not able to fast. You cannot stand it. You are too weak physically. You have had nervous prostration, and you are bordering on a general breakdown, so I ask you, for your own sake and for your parents' sake, to now and here recall that rash vow."

She jumped to her feet and said in a low tone, "Precious father, I love you, I honor you because you are a Christian man; you have set a pious example before your family, but I must say that God has placed this awful burden upon my poor heart, and the Holy Ghost whispered this fast into my soul, and I promise the Triune God and my drunken brother never to swallow another mouthful of food, never to close my eyes again in slumber, until he is saved."

I at once exhorted the people to much prayer. I said to the pastor after the benediction, "We are both strong men. We must fast and pray. We must get under this burden. If the devil can harden this young man, get him the drunker and keep him from the altar and from getting saved, and this girl dies, it will hurt the cause. It will almost lock the doors of the revival. For Jesus' sake, for the young woman's sake, and for that drunken brother's sake, let us betake ourselves to wrestling, agonizing, soul-travail prayer."

We met the young lady in the vestibule the

next morning. She said to us, "The body is weak, but my faith is strong." I met her the second morning. She said, "I am getting weak, but my faith is mounting up." We met her the third morning, and she said, "I'll not meet you in the morning unless my brother gets saved to-day. My body is growing awfully weak." The brother was pouring more red liquor down him; he was cursing, was awfully cross; cursed right in his own home.

The third night, before we preached we were led to have a short testimony service, and the last one to testify was this young lady. She arose and came forward from the choir to the chancel, and as she looked out over that great audience, the tears streaming from her face, she said, "My dear neighbors, friends, kinsmen, pupils, and darling drunken brother, I want you all to hear me, for I believe, honestly believe, that this will be my last testimony in this church. This is the third day I have fasted, and God only knows the heart agony. My body is awfully weak, but I purpose to die before I'll eat or sleep. The Holy Ghost put this on me, and I am going to let Him have His way. I want to say to my drunken brother, who is so drunk on the last pew in this church that he cannot sit up straight, that by to-morrow this time my lips will be closed and my eyes, my hands will be folded across my peaceful breast, and I will be numbered with the dead. I want him to look into my closed eyes and lifeless face, and say, 'Sister died for me.' I want him to have this written on the slab, 'Sister died for me.' " She said, "Friends, it is awful, I feel it is awful. Friends have begged me, the preachers have urged me, to drink some milk, but not one drop, not one bite."

As she closed, she sank into her chair. The young man jumped to his feet. Leaning up against the rear end of the church, he cried out, "My God, sister, I can't stand it. How could I see you dead in the casket! How could I see you go down into the cold grave! I have been miserable for three days, yes, I've been in hell. I have done my utmost to drown conviction, but it has gotten stronger until I can't stand it"—and that young man staggered down the aisle and fell at the altar. That sister threw her arms around him, and such a prayer we never heard before. The young man threw up his hands, and face, and eyes, and oh, how he confessed! How he repented! How he begged God for pardon! How he begged his sister to forgive him! How he begged his parents to forgive him! He jumped from that altar blessedly saved. He grabbed that

sister up in his arms; he ran up and down in the
aisle, pitched her up and caught her like one
would a doll, shouting, "If she hadn't fasted; if
she hadn't prayed; if she hadn't kept at it, I would
have gone to a drunkard's grave and a drunkard's
hell." As they stood in that aisle, his arms
around his sister, he said, "Good people, this woman prayed me through. I felt this was the time,
and my last time. Had she let up I would have
been doomed, lost, damned forever and forever."
They went home that night and had a midnight
supper, and this brother said grace at the table.

This young lady had to cover up her eyes.
She could not look at her father, for he was begging her to cease, to quit. She could not look at
her neighbors, for they said, "It is radical." She
could not look at her kinsmen, for some of them
said, "You'll go crazy." Like Elijah, she covered
up her face, hid her lookers; cried to God for
three long days and nights, *prayed clear through,*
and her drunken brother was gloriously, triumph-
antly saved. We must never look at environments; they cannot help us to pray through; they
cannot inspire us; they can never bring the assurance of the witness, but they may dismay us,
bring doubts and fearful forebodings. Peter
looked at the waves, his surroundings, his envir-

onments, got his eyes off of Christ, and was sinking rapidly to a watery grave when Jesus Christ grasped his hand. Had Peter never looked at the waves, but looked straight ahead, looked at Christ, kept his eyes on the Master, he would have never sunk, never, no, never. His lookers sunk him. His watching the mountain-top waves, sent him down.

CHAPTER XI.

NEVER DISCOURAGED.

1 Kings 18: 42.

The one great barrier in the way, the one clog that Satan puts in the wheel, and the one dark cloud he throws upon the skies, is discouragement. He is well aware of the fact that a discouraged soul is easily defeated. Discouragement places us in the fog, covers the lighthouse, and puts us in troubled waters. Discouragement ices the faith, snows the prayer, and drives us out to sea by a frightful gale. A discouraged man is a weak man, too weak to stand the strain of a siege. To be discouraged is to be blocked about and hedged in by a force that is akin to Hell. Why should we be discouraged? Why should we grow faint-hearted? Why should we stand trembling, knees smiting one the other? Why not be bold?

71

Why not be filled with electric currents of courage? Why not be master of the situation?

Discouragement comes largely through our lookers.

It was in the city of G—— we were conducting a meeting. We had run nine days and nights. It seemed the whole thing was encased in ice, and we were all in the frigid zone. There had hardly been a groan, not a sign of a shout, nor any sign of conviction, so far as one could see. There were only two sanctified people in the church—a man and his wife. We had preached nine long days and nights on Hell. Things were hot. We had stuck to the guns. We had not failed to declare the whole Gospel. We had exhorted and begged the Christians to be much in prayer.

On Monday morning, as we came from the parsonage to the church, we met this sanctified man and his wife, and they were blue. They were actually discouraged. They were down-hearted. They said, "Think of it! We have called you here, a Holiness evangelist, and now we have prayed and fasted, and you have preached, and the ninth day is upon us, and no break. It's awful. We just can't stand it." They said to us, "We can't come to church this morning." We said to them, "The darkest hour is just before dawn. Never be discouraged. Never give up; first, because it is not our work; second, we are not doing it from a selfish viewpoint; third, God knows best how and when to give a revival; fourth, He has promised that His Word should never return unto Him void, and we must look to Him, not to the environments. We must look to Him, not to the hardness of the people. We know that this is one among the most indifferent places in which we have ever preached. The people are so careless, so negligent, so filled with worldly pleasures and amusements, that seemingly they have no desire to give God a chance at their souls, but we must keep at it. We cannot afford to quit, and if we become discouraged we might just as well quit."

We had gone into the woods the evening before, and fallen upon our face and cried to God: "This is an awful battle. Our arms are too short. Thou must do the work. Thou knowest best. Thou understandest that we've done all we saw to be done. Seemingly the saints have prayed. Can this be Thy opportune time? Hear us for Calvary's sake."

We knew perfectly well that God was going to give the revival; we could hear the cows lowing; we could see the mulberry tops shaking. We went on to the church that Monday morning, had several songs and earnest prayers, arose in the pulpit and took our text, raised our hand and started to say something, when, all at once there was a mighty going, there was a mighty rushing wind that filled the house.   One could feel that the Triune God had moved in much of Heaven's artillery; angels seemed to be standing thick in the church; the Shekinah was there.

A stout woman who was sitting in the "Amen Corner," jumped to her feet and said, "Sister Jenkins and I do not speak.   I want you to pray for me."   About that time there was a crash, and this woman was stretched out on the floor, knocked down under the power of God.   A merchant who was a rival to another merchant—they were not on good terms, there was a coolness—arose in the audience, and said, "Mr. Jacobs, if you'll meet me half way we'll bury the hatchet, handle and all."   They started, but behold! they were knocked down in the aisle; they did not get to each other.   A schoolteacher got up to say something, but fell sprawling.   There were thirteen prostrations, and thirty-three running up and down the aisle shouting, and sixteen or seventeen souls swept into the kingdom—when all at once this man and his wife heard the going, and came running into the church. How they did look! They came to us and said, "The walls are falling." We said, "Yes, indeed, God always answers by fire those who stand still and see the salvation of God, and never watch the waves climb the skies and lash the stars, but keep at it, cling on, and pray clear through."

On Sunday night in this revival, twenty rushed to the altar at the first call, twenty came at the second call, and all of the forty were gloriously saved.

This prophet of God knew that for him to let God have His way through him, he must cover up his lookers. How many get discouraged, grow faint-hearted, become dismayed, befogged, do not feel good and well nigh give up, where, if we were to go by faith, sing and work by faith, we would be on the victory side.

A precious woman at Bonnie Camp, who had some kind of spinal spells, had become discouraged. She sent for us, and we took five or six other saints. She had become unconscious when we got to her room. Her head was drawn back, and she was rigid. The husband was wringing his hands and crying; he thought his wife was near the chilly waters of the Jordan. To look at her, one could have had no faith for her healing;

to look at her, one would never have believed for
her healing; to look at her, one would have been
discouraged; to look at her, one would have failed
and have defeated God and a great victory and
her enjoying the blessing of healing. We simply
bowed by the chairs in the room, and first one and
then another prayed. The gurgling sound was
so loud that we thrust our fingers into our ears as
far as we could, and went down in the valley of
earnest, heart agony. The battle raged, but the
saints stuck to the guns; the enemy was entrenched and putting up a stubborn resistance,
but we kept at it.

The Spirit slipped to the writer, saying, "Take
her by the hand and command her, in the name of
Jesus Christ, to arise and walk." Had we looked,
we would never have obeyed this blessed voice;
we would have defeated God's purpose, and this
one, maybe, would have died. We said, "Lord
Jesus, if this is Thy voice, speak once again, and
this Thy servant obeyeth Thee." As quickly as
said, the blessed voice commanded us again to
take her by the hand, and bid her arise and walk.
Stepping to the bedside, we took her by the hand,
saying, "Sister, in the name of Jesus Christ of
Nazareth, we command thee to arise and walk."
Like seventeen hundred bolts of electricity had

struck her body, she jumped clear out over the
footboard of the bed, and ran into the yard, shouting and praising God. Jump? well, I should say
she did! Shout? yes, indeed! It was seeable; it
was knowable; it was real. The great Physician
had come; she had touched, and was made every
whit whole.

It is the enemy's business, and he is ever on
the alert, to carry out this purpose to discourage
God's precious children. He knows that discouragement is one of the greatest channels through
which he can defeat them, and drive them from
the field of victory. The more we study this agent,
this enemy, this channel, the better we understand
how so many good, honest souls are put out of
business; you can listen to their sighs and sobs
and look into their face, and read that they are
under the baneful influence of this treacherous
enemy. He has put a veil over their vision, thrown
clouds upon their future, and made them believe
that there were fearful things for them not far
away on the morrow.

This prophet of God had too much light, lived
too close to God, his prayer life was too sacred,
his hold upon the promise of God was too firm,
to let this bloodhound of perdition tear him from
his base. This prophet got his eyes on God, who

was able to bring strength out of weakness, light out of darkness, wisdom out of ignorance, and a great rain upon the parched earth. This prophet walked on earth, but lived in the skies; he was God's big sunflower; he was fortressed in the riven side of Jesus Christ. This prophet was fully acquainted with the prayer life, and enjoyed it to its fullest extent, and, my reader, if you would only get your eyes on Him who put the sea to sleep, the lightnings and thunders in prison, and saved His apostles from a watery grave, quieted the storm and brought the little bark safely into the harbor, your soul would be fed, your mind at ease, your nerves relaxed, and you would be a walking signboard, ever pointing to what blessed, sweet, real communion will do.

Discouragement takes the blood out of the heart, robs the body of circulation, chills the soul, freezes the river of life, and gives unto us cold hash—when God has a land flowing with milk and honey, burdened with Eshcol grapes, old corn and wine, yea, enough and to spare to make every heart fat, run every cup over, and settle us upon the solid Rock, Christ Jesus. He can establish our feet, making us more than conquerors; and after the giant has fallen, and the smoke of battle has cleared away, we will wake up to the fact that we have only used one stone, and have four more loads in our sling. More than conquerors? Yes, with three hundred God whipped the Midianites and cleared the field of the enemy. One can put a thousand to flight, and two chase ten thousand.

We must ever look to Jesus Christ, and never forget and let our eyes fall on environments not even one time. The God that answered Elijah is the same yesterday, to-day, and forever, the unchangeable God accessible to all humanity. The God that answered Elijah by fire on Mount Carmel is your God to-day, He loves you, and longs to free you, satisfy you, fill and thrill you with His sweet presence.

Discouragement is to the soul what arsenic is to the body; it destroys, it deadens the sensibilities, puts us on the disadvantage ground, and places us at a guilty distance from God. Why be discouraged? Why let the devil get your eyes on the drought? on the dust? on burnt vegetation? Paul says to look unto Jesus Christ, the author and finisher of your faith. If we look heavenward, we see heavenly things, hence, will be encouraged: but to look earthward means discouragement and defeat. Let us look to Jesus, and He will carry us through.

CHAPTER XII.

"BE YE CLEAN."

1 Kings 18: 42.

The time has come; it is here; it is upon us, when God needs a man, a peculiar man—not peculiar because of his own peculiarities or eccentricities, but peculiar because he is peculiarly wholly God's. He is a man, every inch a man; he stands as a man; he walks as a man; he thinks as a man; he acts as a man; he has manly principles; he has convictions born of certainty; he has will power, grit, grace and courage; he has backbone, yea, a column of steel; he has a head that towers above little things, he is too big to live low; he is a man through whom God will be honored. God has been looking for such a man; God has been hunting for such a man, and God has found this man in the person of Elijah. He is bold, fearless, and courageous.

God can send awful conviction upon an entire community through this prophet, and get all
the glory. God can crowd the altar with crying
penitents, and get all the glory. God can give
Hell's artillery crushing defeats, break into the
enemy's lines, spiking his artillery, giving great
revivals, and get all the glory. God can answer
prayer, and through this humble servant of His,
give gracious outpourings of His Spirit until hundreds will be saved and sanctified, and God be
exalted, and man abased.

This is a clean man, a holy man. He preaches
the truth regardless of where the chips fall and
hit; he uncovers sin in high places as well as low;
he hews to the line. He would as quickly thrust
his index finger in the face of King Ahab as not,
crying, "Your corrupt life has brought this apostasy, this fall away, and caused multiplied hundreds, who once had a bright experience, to backslide." He would thrust fiery darts of burning
truth through the black-hearted Jezebel, crying,
"Repent, confess, or burn forever in a devil's
Hell." He shows no one any quarter; seemingly
cares nothing for popularity and public applause;
never dreams of looking in the paper for a report
concerning his meeting, nor watches to see if the
paper put his cut on the first page.

This man is dead to the world, the flesh, and the devil. He is clean, first, in his business life. If a man isn't clean and straight with his fellows, he hasn't a clear wire to Heaven, he could never pray through. For Jones to have cheated Smith out of twenty-five dollars in a trade, or to owe Smith an honest debt of fifty dollars, and fail to make matters right, rushing to the altar, jumping up and professing, would have but little effect upon Mr. Smith; it would be like sleet upon a metal roof; it would drive Smith farther away, and everlastingly block Jones' way of being the channel through which God could reach his neighbor Smith.

If we are not straight with our fellows, how can we expect to be straight with our God?—for God has said, "When thou bringest thy gift to the altar and there rememberest that thy brother hath aught against thee, first—not second, but first; not later, but now—go and be reconciled to thy brother." Your wire is down, forever down, until you make wrong right, crooked straight, black white.

Then second, he is clean in his social life. Here is where we need wisdom, divine wisdom, for all too well we know that the social life needs some salt, a little leaven, much light. It has become corrupted; it is almost a stench in the nostrils of God. For one to turn aside and look in upon the social life, it will almost turn him blind, it will almost stagger his manhood. Things have changed in the last fifty years, they are going to-day at a rapid pace, toward the Niagara of wreck and ruin. For God to answer prayer through us, and use us, we must be clean in every department of our social life; clean in our domestic life. Domestic ties are too sacred, and marriage too divine, to be played with. It would have been a God's blessing if the divorce docket had never been instituted, never heard of. The marriage altar is becoming horribly prostituted, perverted to bad usage. To-day it is not what it was half a century ago. How can a man or woman be God's and think more of anyone else than of his own wife? of anyone else than her own husband? A man must live right every day, if God sends in-wrought prayer into his heart. Many a life has been blasted, many a character wrecked, many a virtuous person dragged into the awful slough of lust, because of unfaithfulness in the domestic life. Trickery here spells damnation later on; trickery here may send one to a suicide's grave; trickery here may cause someone to thrust his or her bony fingers in your face at the Judgment, screaming, "You damned me;" trickery here, turns the hair gray, makes furrows on the face, burns the eyes with scalding tears, saps the soul, and places one in the dark valley of despondency.

We cannot overlook the thought life. "As a man thinketh in his heart, so is he." If a man's thoughts are corrupt, the man's life is always corrupt. The thinker is a dynamo that furnishes electric currents of life; if the thinker is wrong, the whole man is wrong, for, "as a man thinketh, so is he." We backslide first in our head; that is, the wrong kind of thoughts stalk about in the halls of memory; the wrong kind of paintings are thrown upon the mental canvas. A young lady screamed at the altar to the pastor's wife, "My God! my thoughts are as black as Hell; they are lustful thoughts; can God deliver?" For me to be wrong in my thought life, blocks my prayer life; the fountain must be pure, clean, if the water flowing therefrom is healthy and wholesome; the glasses must be clean or the vision will be obstructed.

For me to be endued with Holy Ghost power, for God to entrust a burden to my heart for His work or workers, bespeaks the fact that I must be clean, wholly given up, head, heart and body, to God. A little watching just here will help us.

We cannot keep the birds from flying over our heads, but we can keep the birds from building nests in our hair, laying eggs, and hatching out a brood. You cannot keep thoughts from running through the mind, but never be guilty of asking them to stay overnight, to take dinner with you, or to pay you another visit sometime in the future, for, "as a man thinketh, so is he."

God can, and will, purify our thinker until our thoughts will be heavenly, and we will leave a heavenly influence. We are the cleaner, the stronger, by having clean thoughts. For one to pray clear through, to live in real, vital, close, sweet communion with the Father, Son and Holy Ghost, means that one must be clean in his thought life. Just here is where a great many good souls go down, go down hard. They entertain thoughts, and seemingly enjoy such things, that rob God of His glory, dishonor man, and belittle one's own dignity.

But Elijah was a clean man from every viewpoint; hence God had an unobstructed channel through which to send that great rain upon the parched, burning earth, which quickened the vegetation, sprinkled bright wild flowers through the forest, ladened the atmosphere with fragrant odors, turned a choir of birds loose in the forest, placing a carpet of green upon Mother Earth, and making all nature smile. Had this prophet been anything less than a clean man, the rain could not have come.

A young man once said to the writer: "I have almost been driven to the asylum by hellish thoughts; they have kept me awake all night; they have about wrecked my nerves, and underminded my health. What am I to do?" We said to him, "Fly to God, who was manifested to destroy the works of the devil. Bad thoughts are the works of the devil, therefore Jesus Christ died to destroy these hellish thoughts. Fall upon your face and cry mightily day and night until the fire falls and consumes these awful enemies." Such evil thoughts are injurious to a good, strong mind; they are injurious to a good, strong, healthy, robust body; they are injurious to a sweet, vital, rich experience of know-so, heart-felt, old-time, sin-killing, devil-driving, clear-cut, sky-blue, present salvation from all sin. If He has freed one, He can free two; if He has delivered some, He will deliver all; if He is no respecter of persons, as Elijah was clean there is a possibility of us being clean, and as God wrought mightily through this humble channel, He is desirous of working tremendously through us.

Your community needs a great rain. It would not hurt your church to have a copious shower. Why not besiege Heaven with all your ransomed powers, with all your God-given artillery? Why not keep at it until the thunder peals, the lightning flashes, the clouds rise, and the rain falls? Why not keep at it until the fire falls, the bullocks are eaten up, and the kindlings, all the stones, and the twelve barrels of water are licked up? Why not keep at it until Red Seas open, Jordans give us a dry path, and the towering walls of Jericho bow submissively at our feet? Why not keep at it until the manna falls, quails drop at our tent door, and the stream of water, a great Mississippi, flows through our life? Why not keep at it until lions' mouths are locked, fiery furnaces are quenched, Pentecost is ushered in, and the rushing, mighty wind fills your church and community? Why not keep at it until the Philippian jail takes the Quaker shakes, shakes her doors and shutters from the hinges, the bands and stocks and chains and balls fall from our wrists and ankles, a great light illuminates, and men rush to Christ, crying, "What must I do to be saved?"? Why not keep at it until the whole community knows that we are in the battle? Why not keep at it until God throws a telescope from Heaven

to the Isle of Patmos?   Why not keep at it until
God says, "It is enough; come up higher," and
then sends twenty-four horses of fire, harnessed
in a harness of fire, pulling a chariot of fire, and
we take our seat by the side of Gabriel and Michael, and drive the fiery steeds off through
worlds of fire, and God will say, "Lift up the
gates, ye everlasting doors, and let the kings of
glory come in"?   Then we shall lay down the
cross, take up the crown, play a harp of gold, and
sit down on the banks of Sweet Deliverance with
our loved ones gone on before.   Then, in the
presence of God the Father, Son, and Holy Ghost,
and Heaven's host, we will rejoice, and say,
"Holy! holy! holy!   Thou didst bless us, and we
kept at it, kept at it, kept at it, until this good
hour.   Amen!"

CHAPTER XIII.

IT RAINED.

1 Kings 18 : 42.

This great world of ours was never drier in all its history than at this time. Think of it! there had not been a cloud seen, nor a peal of thunder heard, nor a flash of lightning to illuminate the earth, for three long years and a half; not one drop of rain! not one drop of dew! The great floodgates had been locked, locked tight. Vegetation was literally burned up. Not a bright wildflower to be seen or found; not one green leaf to be seen. The fields were parched and desolate. The dust was thick and like fog in the air. Lowing of cattle, neighing of horses and mules, bleating of sheep, the awful cry of man and beast rent the air with lamentations. No doubt, frightful diseases broke out, for if we were to subtract the water, and have a continuous drought in this

country for three years, oh, the awful diseases!
the stench in the air would be something frightful. The Mississippi River is the life of the
country through which it flows as the blood is the
life of the body. A great drought, then diseases
sweep the country.

Elijah could not afford to look at parched
earth, burnt vegetation; he "placed his face between his knees." He covered up his lookers. He
had the burden. He had the conscious fact that,
in answer to his earnest, wrestling prayer, God
had locked up the skies, and now, through his
earnest, protracted soul agony, God was to unlock the skies and send a gracious rain upon earth.
So Elijah took himself to earnest prayer. The
burden was upon his heart. The time had arrived. It must rain. This man must bring the
rain by praying clear through. He is responsible
if the rain does not fall, for God will send it if he
prays clear through.

He said to his servant, "Go up on the hill and
look off toward the sea and see if there isn't a
cloud." The servant came back and said, "Master, there isn't a sign of a cloud. It is as hot as
ever, and the fog of dust in the air fairly stifles
one. It's awful. It is simply awful. I don't see
how people can stand it much longer." Elijah

said, "Go up on the mountain and look toward the sea and see if there's any cloud." The servant went. He looked and looked, but there was not the slightest sign of a cloud. He came back and said, "Master, it is perfectly clear. I never saw a clearer day in my life, and the sun has never shone hotter. It is blistering hot. My sandals are hurting my feet; my feet are almost blistered." But he said to his servant, "Go up now, look toward the sea." The servant went, and gazed and gazed at the skies toward the sea, but no cloud, not as much as mist. He came back and said, "Master, there is nothing, and I am getting tired—I'm getting hot. I am so thirsty." Elijah said, "Go up now and look." He stood upon the mountain the fourth time and gazed away off toward the sea, but not one sign of a cloud. He came back and said, "Master, there is nothing, and I am awfully tired. We might just as well close this revival. It is useless and fruitless for me to wear out my strength and tire my body in climbing that hill when there is nothing doing. This is a parched district; people have hardened their heart. They have had too much Gospel. We might just as well hang our harps upon a willow. The crowd's not increasing. There isn't any interest manifested, so why wear ourselves out?

Why climb the hill, climb the hill, climb the hill, when there is nothing doing?" But Elijah said, "Go up now, and look toward the sea." For the fifth time he stood upon that mountain—gazing, gazing, gazing, in the far distance toward the sea, and not one single sign, yea, nothing that even had the semblance of a cloud. He came back and said, "Master, not one thing doing. I think it's time we were closing. I think it's time we were going elsewhere."

Well do we remember New Haven, Mo. We had every day covenanted with the people to pray thirty or forty minutes for the revival, for deep, pungent conviction to fall upon the sinners. Nine long days had come and gone, and but little had been accomplished. One night we were impressed at the close of a sermon on Hell, to dismiss the audience and request all to leave the church without a word or a whisper, to leave in deep silence. We knelt at the altar, our head resting upon the chancel. One good old woman in Israel came by and whispered to us, "We are attending the funeral now, but the resurrection will come on the morrow."

She went home; went into her parlor; got on her face and cried out to God, "That preacher is preaching the truth. That preacher is having us to fast and pray. That preacher has had us for nine days to place our hands upon the Bible and covenant that we'd pray thirty or forty minutes each day for a miserable, pungent conviction to seize the sinners, the backsliders, and the ungodly. Lord, if you don't hear, if you will not answer, it will be awful. The devil will throw this in our faces; the sinners will say God doesn't answer prayer." She prayed; she cried all night. About 6: 30 the next morning she got the assurance that a great revival was coming.

That afternoon, Saturday afternoon, we preached from the text for the first time and the last and only time, "And he set a little child in the midst of them." As that woman entered the church that afternoon, she came straight to the pulpit and said to us, "Shout! shout! The walls of Jericho are fallen." At the close of that message fifty or sixty rushed to the altar, and nearly twenty-seven got through good. Saturday night there were 127 at the altar, and a great number were blessedly saved. On Sunday morning the church was packed, and we preached seemingly as never before. What liberty! what unction! what power rested upon the preacher! At the close of the sermon there were about two hundred came to the altar, they fell in the aisles and between the pews. The Presiding Elder crawled across the platform on his knees, took us into his arms, and shouted, "We've never seen it like this before. This is simply wonderful. It is marvelous. Oh, look! look! listen! listen! How they're crying to God!"

Bowed at that altar was this good woman's drunken kinsman, a druggist. She was tremendously interested in him. She had prayed much for him. He got gloriously saved. I tell you God answered that good woman, for she covered up her lookers and would not look at the condition of the church, the hardness of the sinners and indifference of the backsliders, or the awful sins of the community, but she kept at it. She prayed all night, and victory did come, a great victory.

Elijah said, "Go up on the mountain and look toward the sea." The servant went up for the sixth time, and how he gazed! but not a cloud. He came back, saying, "Master, now this is the sixth time, and not one thing doing. Hadn't we better close? I am tired and sleepy. I am almost worn out. My feet are blistered. I never wanted a drink worse in all of my life, and, to tell you the truth, I have looked, looked, looked, until I am discouraged. Let us quit now." Elijah said, "Go up now and look toward the sea." For the seventh

time this servant, this faithful servant, stood upon
that mountain, and as he gazed all at once he saw
something white, yes, a cloud had come out on the
skies. He came running back, shouting, screaming at the top of his voice—how brush cracked
under his feet! He came running to Elijah almost breathless, saying, "Shout! shout! there's a
cloud." Elijah looked up quietly, and said, "My
servant, I knew that. I knew the cloud was coming. I prayed clear through. I had the witness,
the assurance. I was looking to God, not at the
fog of dust; I was listening to God, not to the
voice of man and beast; I was looking to God,
not burnt vegetation; I was looking to God, not
parched surroundings. I knew God, I knew He
would hear and answer prayer."

If we were to wait quietly, patiently, our eyes
on Jesus, our ears stopped up, yea, get into the
closet, God would reward us openly. Our lookers
get us into so much trouble. We are ever too
ready to look and listen to surroundings. We are
so human. O Lord, help us to look to Thee, and
to listen only to Thee, and sweet peace, blessed
soul rest, will crowd the heart, and laden the soul
with that joy that's unspeakable and full of glory.

Elijah never heeded, he never listened to the
voice of his servant. He knew that cloud was

coming; he saw it by the eye of faith, far off.
When God does not answer us at once, that is no
reason why we should let up or let go. Keep at
it. He will answer. Pray clear through. He has
deep, abiding, constant soul rest for every one of
His children. He delights to fill the heart, rest the
soul, and make His service a luxury, yea, a delight. How sweet it is to be in His blessed service when one enjoys the real inwrought prayer
life!

CHAPTER XIV.

Obedience.

1 Thessalonians 5: 22.

The Apostle here gives us one of the greatest Scriptures in the whole library of Divine truth. In it we have a command, a prayer and a promise, and upon obedience to this command hinges the destiny of mankind. To disobey this injunction, is to go down with the wicked and defeated; to obey, is to have success, and the presence of the Triune God. To disobey is to be driven by frightful impressions, and the agents of Hell, into the pit; to obey is to have the angels of God encamp around about you, to have vital communion with the Father, to be master of every circumstance, and to come off more than conqueror through Christ Jesus.

"Abstain from all sights of evil." Had David obeyed this injunction, he would have escaped that awful crash, that multiplied defeat, that awful murder, the disgracing of his own daughter, the killing of his own son by a brother, the dying of the illegitimate child, and his crying, "The pangs of hell have gat hold upon me," under the blazing sermon sent by the Holy Ghost through that fiery preacher Nathan, from that memorable text, "Thou art the man!"

Had Samson obeyed this command, he would never have gotten up a flirtation with Delilah, lost connection with the skies, lost his locks and his eyes, and pulled the mill-sweep like an ox. Look once at Samson, the mightiest preacher God ever pitted against Hell's artillery. No doubt angels crowded the galleries of the skies and watched Samson with the jawbone of an ass clean up a thousand devils and put to flight the armies of Hell. What a preacher! What a soul-saver and power for good! How the Spirit did at times swoop down upon him! He was the army, the infantry, the cavalrymen, the captain, the major, the general; and when this mighty man of God went on the warpath others trembled. But, alas! oh, how sad! I can hear the sobs and sighs now when that awful message went through to the skies, "Samson has fallen." The devil chuckled and laughed; all Hell ha! ha'd!

Why did it happen? First, because Samson did not "abstain from all sights of evil;" Samson did not resist the first glance, the first look. Second, because Samson did not walk in the light God had given. Third, because Samson did not fortress his weak point. Fourth, because he doubtless went on past success. Fifth, because he failed to live wholly in the will of God. Sixth, because he got out of Divine order. When a man gets out of Divine order, defeat is his sad fate. God cannot and will not endorse covering up sin. "Be sure your sin will find you out." "Abstain from all sights of evil."

One's thought life must be pure, for "as a man thinketh in his heart, so is he." The heart is the seat of government, hence if the government is not pure every channel will become more or less corrupted. Tell me your thoughts, and quickly I can tell you your life. Abstain from devilish fancied imaginations. The imagination is a fruitful channel, and if dedicated to God, sanctified to His glory, will become a very useful channel through which God may be glorified, and you become a fruitful tree in His vineyard; but if the imaginations are turned over to the devil, and allowed to harnass up these God-given channels, woe be unto you! Look out! David will hang his harp upon the willow; Samson will lose his locks. One ounce of prevention is worth tons of cure; a stitch in time will save nine. These are true old adages. They are brimful of truth, and had mankind heeded their admonition, David would not have gone down with a crash, Samson would not have committed suicide. When one fails to walk in the light, when one fails to obey God, there is danger ahead, for if one gets out of Divine order and becomes disconnected from the skies, what will the end be? Look at Samson! Look at Saul! If we are not in Divine order, we must be disobedient, and how can God bless and sanction a disobedient child?

"Abstain from all sights of evil." This means fleeing from wrong. A good run is much better than a bad stand. If one should see a rattlesnake crawling toward a precious baby sitting out in the grassy yard, there would be one of two things to be done; we could rush and pick the child up in our arms and flee, or grab up a hoe and kill the snake; but if we knew we could not kill the snake, we could grab the child up and skip. Why wait? why watch and see just how close you can allow that snake to get to the child before you grab the child? If you see a mad dog coming into your yard, will you wait until it comes within a few

short feet of the child? Will you wait until it;
fastens its teeth in the child's clothes? No, you.
flee to the child, grab it and run back into the;
house, locking the door and screaming for help. .

We must not, under any circumstances, look
upon sin long. We mean by long, gaze upon it.
You cannot keep from seeing things, but you can;
keep from gazing. David doubtless could not;
have kept from seeing Mrs. Uriah, but he could
have kept from peeping and gazing through the.
window. The second he saw her, if he would on-.
ly have turned and said, "O Lord, keep this thy,
servant," angels would have flown thick and fast;
around him, unctuous power would have come,
upon him, and a great victory would have been his
to enjoy. But perhaps David stood a bit and;
gazed until the animal nature took possession of;
him, and he committed the awful sin of adultery,
and brought the awful, withering, blasting disap-
proval of God upon his household.   i

You should remember and never forget that
the iniquities of the parents are visited down to
the second, third and fourth generations.
Here is where the innocent must suffer with the
wicked. Therefore, how carefully ought parents
to live. Their thoughts should be clean, their
imaginations pure, their language chaste, and

their lives above reproach. If you want a good, robust child, a child of character, begin seventy-five years before it is born. Character is not made in a day; character is what men *are*.

If we should "abstain from every sight of evil," what experiences we would enjoy! what beautiful, perfect love would leap through our hearts on its musical, triumphant course! what singing birds would flit through the woodland of our soul, warbling their beautiful songs of joy! Our hearts would be laden with the fragrant odors from God's promises. One cannot keep these ugly imaginations from flitting through the mind. None of us can keep the birds from flying over our heads, but who need be so foolish as to let them build a nest in his hair? When these ugly thoughts come, keep them on the run. Do not take their hat and coat; do not give them a chair; do not furnish them a bed. They are rebels; and you must conquer and put down a rebellion.

Paul is praying for the Thessalonians, who were abstaining from all sights of evil, who were rejoicing all the time, and constantly in the spirit of prayer, to be wholly sanctified. Paul is praying for a wide-awake, regenerated crowd; a crowd that had peace with God; a crowd that had family

prayer, and grace at their table; a crowd that
lived right moment by moment. They spoke to
everybody; there was no hatred in their hearts,
no malice or strife, no bickering or backbiting, no
tongue-lashing.

Remember, folks who are cold, lukewarm,
careless, indifferent, in reclamation or regencra-
tion, are not the ones who enter into sanctification, but those who are walking in all the light He
has given them. Remember, the work of sanctification is wrought by God the Father, Son and
Holy Ghost. It is a definite work in the heart of
the true believer who has abandoned his all and
presented his body a living sacrifice. How easy
for one who is right with God, living in the sunshine of God's will, to look up and believe. "Ask,
and ye shall receive; seek, and ye shall find; knock,
and it shall be opened unto you."

Sanctification does not only qualify one for
service, but places that beautiful grace of perfect
love in the heart; and it eradicates the "old man,"
destroys the works of the devil, and places one in
that beautiful relationship to God that none but
the pure in heart enjoy, and then we have peace
with all men.

CHAPTER XV.

PERSEVERANCE IN PRAYER.

"And straightway Jesus constrained his disciples to get into a ship, and go before him unto the other side, while he sent the multitudes away.

"And when he had sent the multitudes away, he went into a mountain apart to pray: and when the evening was come, he was there alone." (Matt. 14: 22, 23.)

The incidents and historic facts clustering about this Scripture are marvelous. First, the great multitude crowding into the desert place with their sick, to hear the Christ tell the wonderful story of redemption. The multitude was unprepared, from the viewpoint of eatables. The people grew hungry, and must have something to eat. The disciples informed the Master that there was not a thing on the ground to eat, save five loaves and two fishes. Jesus looked upon the mul-

titude with tender compassion, took the five loaves
and two fishes, and blessed the same. The great
multitude was fed, appetite appeased, and twelve
baskets full of fragments left.

Jesus felt the necessity of prayer. He knew
it was time for Him to get alone, to get away from
His disciples, away from the multitude. He must
make way for secret prayer. Hence, He constrained His disciples to get into the ship and go
before Him unto the other side, while He sent the
multitudes away. If He had not sent the disciples
away, the multitudes would have stayed, for
where the carcase is, there will the eagles gather.
When the disciples were gone, and the multitudes
were gone, He went up on the mountain alone in
prayer.

We watch this lone figure as He climbs that
mountain, drops of sweat running down His face;
His cheeks were red, His bosom heaving, His
breath short, but by the projecting rocks and
shrubbery He pulls Himself on up that mountain-
side. He left the great multitudes, He tore Himself away from His disciples, He climbed the rugged mountain-side, and yonder, on top of that
mountain, He was alone with His Father. He
made way for prayer.

If we ever do anything worth while for Jesus,

we must make way for much secret prayer, we must tear ourselves away from the duties of home and loved ones, and get alone with Jesus daily. Well do we remember when we entered college, a poor boy, with no money and no backing. The devil said to us, "You must pray little and work long and hard, for you are going on borrowed capital, interest will eat you up, and you can pray when you get through school." How cunning the devil was. We woke up to the fact in a few weeks that we were going to lose out unless we prayed more. To make way and time for prayer, we fasted every Wednesday morning and every Friday morning. The first Wednesday morning we had not been on our knees three minutes until the devil said, "You must be fair with your room-mate; you clean out the bowl, fill the pitcher, empty the ashes, make up the beds and clean up the room, while he's at breakfast." Soon we were cleaning the bowl and carrying out the ashes, when we woke up to the fact that we might just as well have gone to breakfast, for we were not getting to pray any more by fasting, so we said, "Splitfoot, get behind us; we mean to stay on our knees one hour, no matter how the room looks, we are going to pray one hour. We are fasting this morning. We've made this time. We've set aside this hour for nothing else but prayer."

The devil will send in visitors or neighbors, ring the doorbell, ring the telephone—send around something to beat you out of your secret prayer.

The Master stayed upon the mountain until three o'clock in the morning, then went from the mountain-top to the storm-tossed vessel and frightened disciples, and saved them from a watery grave, and delivered Peter from the mad waves of that frightful typhoon.

The pentecostal crowd went from that ten-days prayer-meeting out upon the streets of Jerusalem, preached a few moments, shouted and sang and testified, and three thousand ran to the mourner's-bench and were brightly saved that glad day. Mark you, they went from the ten-days prayer-meeting! Mordecai and Esther went from their knees, after three days and nights of fasting and prayer, and the Jewish race was saved. Nineveh was spared after the king and all the inhabitants of that great metropolis had gotten in ashpans, covered themselves with sackcloth, and prayed clear through. The fire that God had stacked up to pour out upon that wicked city was locked up by way of answer to the earnest cries of that people. The clouds came out, and the great rain fell, earth was blessed, man and beast watered, after Elijah had placed his face between his knees, and prayed clear through.

If Jesus Christ, our Savior, the Son of God, saw and felt the need of whole nights of prayer, and took Himself away from a tremendous congregation and His loving disciples to make way for prayer, how much more do we finite creatures need to tarry, wait before God, in much earnest, protracted soul travail!

We too often fail to make way and take time to pray; we are in too big a hurry; we are always on the run; our hands are full, our heads crowded, our feet sore, by running hither and thither. We work, work, work. We organize this society and that society, plan this and start that. We go to Sunday services tired, come back Sunday night fagged. We are not growing much in grace. We are living at a poor dying rate. We get up in class-meeting too often, and say, "Brethren, I'm having a hard time. The roads are slippery, quite rough; the mountains are high, the clouds are dark. I'm not having a good time serving the Lord. Pray for me that I may hold out faithful." No wonder children do not want religion after hearing parents talk like this in the house of God.

If we were to have time (and we must take time)
to pray, if we had our secret devotions, prayed
clear through on our knees, we would go forth delivering, scattering sunshine, and our lives would
be very fruitful. The work in His cause would
be delightful, enjoyable. The friction would be a
thing of the past. The laboriousness would take
wings, and we would work and be rested. How
eagerly we would go to His house! How refreshed
we would come home!

Prayer is the oil that lubricates the machinery,
that causes all to run smoothly; no hot boxes, no
breaking of belts, no slipping of cogs, no leaking
of steam, no water to put out the fire. Prayer,
prayer by the hour, daily prayer, a continuous
spirit of prayer, much secret prayer, makes the
Christian life a golden sunbeam, turns the birds
loose in the soul, causes the flowers to bloom, the
joy-bells to ring. It makes the worship of God
easy.

One lady said to another, "Why is it you go
to church joyful, and work anywhere there's an
open door, come back home happy, and rejoice all
week? Why is it you sit and read the Bible so
much? Why is it your face has the shine?" The
good woman said, "I have been praying daily for
seven years, not less than one hour a day. That

is the answer to your question." A little boy once
said, "My mamma's the best woman in the world."
Someone said, "Why?" "Because she goes in her
prayer-room with her Bible, and cries and talks
to the man Jesus a long time every day." A young
man came in one night from a dance. Hearing
the sobs of his mother after midnight, the Holy
Spirit said, "You are breaking that mother's
heart." That mother slipped to his room, slipped
her arms around the boy, hot tears falling into his
face. She said, "My precious son, mother's been
praying hours to-night for you. I'm afraid the
devil is leading you Hellward in a hurry." The
young man placed his arms about his mother and
said, "Mother, your prayers are answered; I'll
never go to another dance." God heard the midnight cries of this broken-hearted mother. It
pays to pray. It pays to live upon one's face.
Prayers change the tide, and cause things to go
God's way.

From the human viewpoint, it looked like Daniel would be eaten up by the lions, but he had spent
much time in prayer; hence, God delivered. It
looked like Elijah would starve to death out there
under the juniper-tree, but he had spent much
time on Mount Carmel in prayer, and the fire had
fallen, backslidden Israel had been reclaimed, and

Baal's false prophets killed; hence, God's angel woke Elijah up under the juniper-tree, and said, "Here is food; eat." Elijah ate heartily, pillowed his head upon his arm, slept and rested, woke up and ate another good meal, and went forty days in the strength thereof. Cornelius prayed much. He was hungry for holiness of heart. He had cried through to God. He had begged God to send one Holiness preacher his way. Here came the sanctified evangelist, Peter; a great revival broke out, and Cornelius and his household swept into the fountain.

Prayer, midnight prayer, a constant spirit of prayer, will unlock Heaven's gates and flood the soul with satisfaction. John prayed on the Isle of Patmos, and behold, the telescope of prophecy was swung in place, and John had a peep into Heaven that he could never have had but for the Patmos experience.

The most enjoyable experience a Christian ever can have is to be alone with God in prayer. There is where His will is revealed concerning you and your work. There is where plans are launched for your good and His glory. God knows best for us and what we are qualified best for, what line of work we will be most successful in, but we cannot get into it save through the

prayer life. Prayer makes work easy. Prayer
gives us freedom, freedom with God and freedom
before man. It unlocks our mouths, frees our
opinions, and gives us an atmosphere of whole-
someness. Jesus spent many nights in prayer,
and just after these nights in prayer He did some
tremendous work. When He came from the
Mount of Transfiguration, He delivered the man's
son from the devil, when the disciples had failed.
When Jesus came from the mountain to the
storm-tossed waters He delivered Peter from the
mad waters which would have swallowed him up.
The great work God is accomplishing through
His agents for the salvation of a lost world is
wrought through men and women of much protracted prayer.

A man on a steamer once asked a great preacher why he had such tremendous success. The
young preacher, with a heart filled with perfect
love, said, "Sir, God keeps me on my face." The
sexton heard a great preacher in his study one
Sabbath morning, begging very earnestly for
someone to go with him into the church. The
sexton went back the second time, and the pastor
was still pleading. Soon the preacher walked out
into the pulpit; his face was all aglow, the power
of the Most High was resting upon him. He

preached, and twenty souls rushed to the altar and
were converted that morning.   That preacher
came from his knees to the pulpit.   Someone asked
a preacher after he had preached a great sermon,
and over a hundred were at the altar, why the success?   A friend said, "That preacher prayed all
night.   He never retired."

Now, if we know, and see, and feel the great
importance of prayer, has not God turned in light,
and can we retain our relationship to God as a
son or daughter, and fail to walk in this light, fail
to pray, fail to have regular times to go to Him
in secret prayer?   Have you ever blocked the way
of a sweeping revival in your community or church
by a prayerless life?   Have you ever defeated God
in saving some of your loved ones by neglecting
prayer?   Have you wondered why the fire hasn't
fallen, awful conviction seized the sinners, and
men crowded the altar?   Have you ever taken the
almanac and counted how long it had been since
you had a good, sweet, real enjoyable season of
prayer?   Why don't you enjoy religion to-day as
you once did?   Why aren't you as happy to-day
as you were the day you were converted?   Doesn't
one grow in grace?   What is the matter?   Oh,
yes, you've let up in your prayer life.   You are too
busy to pray.   You can't take the time away from

other pressing duties and give it to this all-important duty, prayer. No wonder our hearts are empty and our spirits weak, and we grow faint and get scared at the first crack of the gun. No wonder we are midgets, no wonder we pant for breath. Why, the soul is fed through prayer, and it gets more strength through prayer than from any other exercise in a religious life. When we fail to pray, we starve the soul. When we fail to pray, we lessen our possibilities, give the devil the vantage ground, and place God at a disadvantage. When we fail to pray, we water our fire, break our belts, and give Satan the leverage. Let us wake up now, and betake ourselves to more earnest prayer. One has said, "I cannot remember that I ever prayed a soul through to God. I do not remember that I ever prayed a revival into my community. I do not remember that I ever had the conscious fact that I had prayed clear through. In fact, I am a little confused about my experience. I'm not quite certain; I hope I am right, but there's a doubt."

Doubts come in when we let up in prayer. Fears stalk about in the soul when the briars grow up in our prayer-meeting path. If we would have grit, grace, and backbone, we must pray. If we would be fat and healthy, we must pray. If we would have the rich experience and do things worth while for God and lost humanity, like other saints, we must pray. Let us never let up nor let go until we know really that we have placed the key of prayer in the lock of Heaven, and turned it, and the great door has opened, and the rivers of pleasures are flowing into our heart.

CHAPTER XVI.

God Will Take Care of You.

"Now when Daniel knew that the writing was signed, he went into his house; and his windows being open in his chamber toward Jerusalem, he kneeled upon his knees three times a day, and prayed, and gave thanks to God, as he did aforetime." (Daniel 6: 10.)

This passage discloses one of the great prayers of the Old Testament Scriptures. He was a man of rare character, a great mind and a rich experience. He was living in the full light of a full redemption. He was walking in all the light the Holy Spirit had turned in upon his pathway. He was a man who did not serve God spasmodically. He did not have religious spasms. We mean by this he did not get into a series of meetings, listen to special lines of preaching, get under a tremendous conviction, and vow and promise

God to do so and so, and then never do it. Too many of us get worked up in a revival without getting the "old man" worked out of us; hence, too often, and too soon after the revival closes, we close down the mill, it ceases to grind, we lose our zeal, and hang our harps upon the willows.

We oftentimes make statements and vows in a series of meetings that are hurtful. Why? Because people watch us and see that we do not follow up and follow out what we have vowed and promised. Here is a young lady who gets worked up in a meeting, and tremendously burdened for China. She gets up before a crowded house, with a shining face and tear-filled eyes, clapping her hands for joy, telling her neighbors and kinsmen that she will soon be in China, and in less than twelve months she is married and settled down. Here is a young man who gets wrought up spasmodically, jumps up and declares that he has been called to preach the Gospel, then in a few short months we hear no more of his call.

Daniel had ballast, road-bed. He was a stalwart character. He did not get into a revival, get worked up, promise God a tenth, then soon cool off, pocketing every "brownie." When Daniel made a statement, he lived up to it. He did not change his manner of living at all when the king

sent forth a decree that all men bow the knee, that
every knee should bow before the statue. Daniel
went home, threw up his windows, and bowed with
his face toward Jerusalem three times a day, "as
he had done aforetime." Mark you carefully the
"aforetime"; that is to say, Daniel had been praying three times a day all of his religious life. He
lived right every day; he prayed clear through
every day; he had the burden of prayer, the spirit
of prayer, the liberty of prayer. He lived upon His
knees, and when these awful tests came his anchor
held. He was rooted and grounded. He was not
driven by a mad gale. He was not caught off of
his base. Daniel knew, and knew full well, that
God would take care of him. Why? Because of
his faithfulness; because of his constant watch-
fulness; because he lived upon his face.

A praying man, one who *really prays,* one who
has the spirit of prayer, is hard to put to flight, is
on his guard. He has his pickets out. You remember that God said "watch" as well as "pray."
W-A-T-C-H comes first. A praying man is a
watchful man. The enemy cannot swoop down
on him and catch him napping.

The reason why our prayers do not reach the
Throne and bring the desired answer is, we do not
live up to our privileges and opportunities; we do

not hug the firing-line and toe the mark; we do
not walk in all the light God gives us; hence, when
we go to prayer we go as weaklings. We are
made weak by weak living. We get sleepy, tired,
feel sluggish, have no spirit of prayer, no energy;
then we do not get a grip upon God. A good
liver—and it takes a mighty good liver to be a
good pray-er—can pray right. No man can pray
the fires out of Heaven unless he lives right; lives
right in his home, before his wife and children; ir-
ritableness, crossness, and all harsh-speaking are
things of the long by-gones. For a man to pray
clear through he must, indeed, be a good liver
before his own family. One will have a hard
time in prayer when he does not live right in his
own home before his own family.

Daniel lived right. His family knew that he
lived right. His neighbors felt his righteous life.
He had fruits. There was not a barren tree in
his orchard. Every tree was loaded with luscious,
ripe fruit. If we live right all the time, it will be
easy for us to pull the fires out of Heaven during
a revival, and point sinners to Calvary. One of
the things that is hurting God's cause is a prayerless life; that is, a life minus prayer; that is, a life
without prayer. When tests come, the praying
man is ready. He is manned with heavy artillery.

He has his fortresses and rifle-pits ready. We would rather be a great pray-er than a great preacher; we would rather be a great pray-er than a great singer, for it is the prayers of the righteous that avail much.

Let us take ourselves to more earnest, protracted seasons of prayer. Let us be careful to have, every day, secret prayers. If you want a fat soul, a healthy soul, a joyful soul, *pray much.* If you want a strong, robust faith; a deep, sweet, rich experience, *pray much.* If you want to live on the sunny side of the street, *pray much.* If you want to keep out of Satan's dumps, *pray much.*

CHAPTER XVII.

Daniel's Grip upon God.

Daniel 6: 10.

The historic facts that cluster about this text disclose the fact that Daniel had a grip upon God. He was a fearless man, a man without fear. He had no man-fearing and no man-pleasing spirit. He dared to do the right; he dared to follow God; he dared to walk in all the light the Holy Ghost shed upon his pathway. He was a courageous man. He was a man who stood flat-footedly upon the immutable Word of God, and the gates of Hell could not prevail against him. The clouds were dark; the lightnings were flashing from one dark mountain range of cloud to another; the peals of thunder from Hell's artillery seemingly were jarring the very foundation stones of Mother Earth. It was dark, awful dark—so black that one without a grip upon God could not see which way to go. The winds were blowing at a terrific gale; the waves were leaping skyward, but Daniel had his compass and square, he knew his longitude and latitude. He understood how far he had traveled, and the speed he was making; hence, God had the advantage, and Daniel's anchor held fast.

The decree had gone forth that every man must bow the knee to the statue. This was done by the enemies of Daniel to entrap him. They saw in this clean, holy man of God nothing through which offence could be taken, but they must bring charges concerning his religious life. Therefore this hellish decree. But Daniel stood —stood like a Pike's Peak; stood like the rock of Gibraltar, and you know the waves dashing and lashing the rock of Gibraltar only keep it clean, and through these crucial tests, these long tunnels, these dark tunnels, these deep gorges and sore afflictions, we are made more like God, and grow stronger, and become better qualified to live in the center of His will and do exploits for our Master.

A praying man is forearmed for battle; that is, he is prepared beforehand; that is, he has his artillery shining, his heavy guns manned. He understands what to do, and best how to do it, for a praying man has the ear of God. He has vital connection with the skies. His telephone wires are in good condition. He has splendid connection. Hence, the man who lives upon his face can soon get the mind of God, but be it understood, just because you can't pray through in a minute, or an hour, or a day, or a week, is no argument why you should not continue wrestling in heart agony, for if we continue and faint not, we shall reap, for the bread cast upon the waters will return not many days hence. The trouble with us is we do not pray long enough; we do not live long enough upon our faces. Thirty minutes seems a long time; we get so tired; we yawn, stretch ourselves, and say, "This thirty minutes is the longest I have ever experienced." Why? Because we are not in close touch with the skies: hence, we haven't the liberty in prayer; we haven't the freedom; it is burdensome; we are tired; we can't someway, somehow, get into a spirit of prayer. One should pray, and keep praying, and never stop praying until he really gets into the spirit of prayer. The devil is ever on hand to retard every possible advancement in the prayer life. He is too well aware of the fact that the prayers of the righteous avail much, that God hears the effectual, fervent prayer. He knows that Elijah prayed the fire out of Heaven, and through every agent possible he will break into your prayer life to hinder, to cause you to jump from your knees about the time you are getting audience with God. One should be so concerned that he will not allow anything to take him from the sweet hour of prayer.

If you want to live in clouds—that is, have your experience cloudy—pray little. If you enjoy living in the dumps, having doubts and fears within, pray little. If you can revel in the dark valley of despondency, pray little. If you want a hard road to travel, a rocky road, filled with disappointments, pray little. If you want defeats and no victories, all downs and no ups, pray little. If you want to live on the shady side of the street, fuming with peevishness and fretfulness, pray little. If you want a long-faced religious experience, to be poutish, cross, pray little. If you want your children to go into the paths of sin, pray little. The great trouble to-day with Christendom is a lack and failure to pray clear through. Praying is not an easy task; praying is not like sitting down and having a chat with a friend. One must take time to pray, special time to pray and stay upon his knees until he gets victory. Getting down and getting up before victory comes breeds doubts. Let us betake ourselves to a spirit of earnest, protracted seasons of prayer.

CHAPTER XVIII.

TAUGHT BY THE HOLY GHOST.

Daniel 6: 10.

Daniel knew how to pray, because he was taught by the Holy Ghost. Natural man does not know how to pray, nor can he teach himself. Hence, he needs the Holy Ghost to pray through him with groanings which cannot be uttered by lips of clay. One of the disciples said, "Lord, teach us to pray as John also taught his disciples," and Jesus said, "It is expedient that I go away, that the Holy Spirit may come, who will bring all things to your remembrance."

The Holy Ghost will help our infirmities, for we are not fighting against flesh and blood, but we are fighting against principalities and powers. Remember that Satan's force is a strong force. and this force is led by the prince of the power of the air.

"Praying always with all prayer and supplication in the Spirit, and watching thereunto with all perseverance and supplication for all saints; and for me, that utterance may be given unto me, that I may open my mouth boldly, to make known unto you the mystery of the gospel, for which I am an ambassador in bonds: that therein I may speak boldly, as I ought to speak." We see here that the Christian's foe is a powerful one, and there is only one way to defeat this foe, that is, by praying always with all prayer and supplication in the Spirit. The Holy Ghost will teach us how to pray; He will lead us out into prayer; He will place burdens of prayer upon our hearts; He will place the earnest spirit of prayer in our soul. He knows the enemy; hence, He knows how to gird us for the battle, how to qualify us for a victorious service, how to gird us for the battle's front, how to prepare us for the bugle's blast.

Daniel cleaned up the enemy and cleared the field of the foe by throwing up his windows and praying three times a day as he had done aforetime, and we are taught, by this great man's example, that if we are to be victors, glorifying the name of Jesus Christ and gathering precious sheaves into His garner, it will be accomplished only through prayer.

George Mueller housed, fed and clothed multiplied thousands of orphans, by living upon his knees. A. B. Simpson, who prayed all night at Old Orchard, Me., in earnest, wrestling prayer, the next morning took up over one hundred thousand dollars for missionary purposes. Why? Because he prayed clear through that night. The Holy Ghost unctionized him, the Holy Ghost filled him with the spirit of prayer. He had soul agony, soul travail. He got the answer. He knew the money was coming.

The saints who live upon their faces know beforehand that victory is theirs. What confidence, what settledness, what contentment, there is in the heart of those who have a grip in prayer! What sweet peace floods the soul, what joyful songs leap through the avenues of the heart! The choir of birds is turned loose in the forest of one's spirit, warbling the sweet songs of joy; the flowers are blooming, ladening the air with fragrant odors; the leaping brooklets run across the sparkling pebbles of one's soul, carrying a freshness of peace that is full of glory and sunshine.

There is a rest in God, a rest of faith, a rest of mind, a rest of body, a sweet rest, deep rest, abiding rest, undisturbed rest, a rest that brings mastery, self-mastery. We are conquerors, yea, more than conquerors, through much continued, earnest prayer. If you would live on the mountain of Beulah, and be swept by one holy gale after another, of God's perfect love, live much on your knees. If you would be strong in faith, robust in experience, have that constant, intimate relationship with God that Daniel had, *pray.* God needs pray-ers, more pray-ers. We would rather be a great pray-er than a great preacher; we would rather be a great pray-er than a great man, for it is the pray-ers that pull the fire out of Heaven, put a withering, blistering conviction upon sinners, crowd the altars with earnest seekers who confess, uncover, and pray right through to God.

Have you ever had the Holy Ghost to place some soul hard upon your soul, and cause you to fly to your room, upon your face, and cry and wrestle over that soul? Has God sent your community a gracious, soul-saving revival, through your prayers? Mordecai and Esther fasted and prayed, yea, wrestled in prayer, they had heart agony and soul travail, and in answer to their earnest, protracted prayer, God sent one of the greatest revivals the Jewish race ever witnessed. He delivered the entire race through Mordecai's and Esther's prayers. Another time, the Holy Ghost came in His sanctifying power upon the hundred and twenty after they had had a prayer-meeting for ten days.

We have never had any trouble in having sweeping revivals where the saints had been earnestly praying for weeks ahead of the revival. A certain lady once said to this preacher, "I had the witness for one hundred souls three months before you began the meeting in Glasgow, Ky." The reason there are not greater revivals and more souls saved is, the saints do not pray things through. God has said, "Ask, and ye shall receive." He has said, where two or three agree as touching any one thing, He will be in the midst. Let us be certain that our hands and skirts are free from the blood of men; let us be certain that no one stumbles over our prayerless life, into Hell. I tell you it is awful when we think of the prayerless lives in every community, men and women who profess to love God and their families, and yet have not vital connection with God in their prayer life. They enjoy the daily paper, the chats with friends, but when it comes to the real prayer life, they are ignorant. These things ought not so to be!

CHAPTER XIX.

AN HONEST MAN.

Daniel 6: 10.

This is a great verse, one of the most wonderful verses in the Bible. It discloses the fact that there lived a man who was honest, pure, sober, truthful and upright to the core. He feared God, and answered every roll call, obeyed every injunction, and lived up to all the light given him by the Holy Ghost. He was fearless. He did not cool off, let up or let down when the frightful decree was heralded forth that anyone who failed to bow the knee to the king's statue would be thrust into the den of lions. There was not one bit of fear, not the slightest wave that played over this honest, sincere, holy heart. He was as fearless as God could make man.

After reading the hellish decree he went home, threw up his windows—mark you! he did not do one thing that he had not been doing; did not put on one extra; did not pray any louder, but only did what he had been doing aforetime. Mark well the "aforetime." He had been having his family prayers; he had been having them with open windows; he had been having them with his face toward Jerusalem; and when this awful crash came, he kept doing what he had been doing aforetime.

God will always take care of such a man. God will never see such a man trodden under foot. God has always delivered those who lived as Daniel lived. If we would have success, we must live where God can give us success. Crowded altars, scores and scores being saved and sanctified, can only be given to those who live in constant touch with the skies. Now, you may say, "I know some who are black sheep, and yet they have some success." That is true. God will bless His own Word, no matter through what channel it may go, but, mark you well, the black sheep do not have great break-downs and sweeping revivals constantly. Some we know, and sorry are we in our heart that we know them, who are living in sin, covered-up sin, and yet they go right on preaching the Word, and sometimes souls get through to God in their meetings. But in their hearts they have no connection with God in prayer; they do not enjoy the sweet, deep, blessed communion with God. They pray but little, for if they did, light would be turned in.

Daniel had power to get audience with God. Why? He had had audience with God. There had been no break, and when this awful storm swept down upon this holy man of God, he stood firmly because he stood only in the will of God. We have seen good men, holy men, praying men, who, if it had not been for their grip in prayer, would have been swept from their feet, and if they had not been prayed up, had not lived up, would have been swept out by a mad gale. Elijah was prayed up before the great Mount Carmel sacrifice. Moses was prayed up before God gave him the Decalogue. Joshua was prayed up when he marched around the walls of Jericho.

Notice, every man through whom God has wrought mightily has been a man of much prayer. Luther prayed three hours a day. Knox prayed by the hour. Fletcher was a man of much soul travail. Spurgeon lived upon his face. Madame Guyon was a woman of constant prayer. If we would do something for God and lost humanity, we must be earnest in our prayer life. The greatest victory that comes to one usually comes after a protracted season of prayer. The fire fell after Elijah had prayed; the rain fell after Elijah had placed his face between his knees; the great deliverance came to the Jewish race after Mordecai and Esther had fasted and prayed three days and three nights; the great pentecostal fire came rushing upon the hundred and twenty in the upper room after they had prayed ten days; the scales fell from Paul's eyes after he had prayed three days and nights.

Prayer is the channel through which we reach the haven of rest. Prayer is the channel through which God enters into the soul. Prayer is the wire over which comes the blessed news, freedom from sin. Let us remember, always remember, and never forget, that prayer is the key that unlocks Heaven. Hence, we should stay upon our knees, wrestle, agonize, fast, pray clear through. Be determined to place the key in the lock.

CHAPTER XX.

Not An Easy Task.

Daniel 6: 10.

Praying clear through as Daniel did is not an easy task. It is one of the hardest battles to be fought. It is one of the hardest conflicts in one's life. It takes grit, grace, and backbone. It draws out more physical energies, more mental quickness, more spiritual unction than any other exercise in one's religious life. It is easy to sing; most anyone can sing. There is not much art in singing. All one needs to know is the notes and understand the scale of music. It is an easy thing for one to preach when he is called and has a message, preaching is easy. It is delightful. Testifying is certainly a joyful service. It does not take much strength to testify. One just has to get up and begin telling the sweet story, and it rolls forth, but when you come to prayer, the devil and all his forces are on hand to impede your progress, thwart your pathway, yea, to cause your cogs to slip, your engine to leak steam, and its water to put out the fire. The devil knows that if he does not break into an earnest spirit of prayer something is going to happen, something is going to be doing. His plans will be frustrated, his agents put to flight, his territory conquered: hence, he puts forth his best agents to block the pathway of prayer.

Over there in Daniel, when he was praying earnestly, praying long, praying in heart agony, the devil withstood the angel who had been sent from God with an answer to Daniel's prayer, twenty-one long days, three weeks, but Daniel kept at it. He never let up; he never quit; he knew it was on the road; he knew darkness must be broken up, the clouds must rift, the sunshine must break through, for if he failed to pray clear through, defeat would be his, God be dishonored, the cause injured, and Daniel's experience hurt, so Daniel took the thing by the job. He put out his pickets; he went into battle never to let up until victory rolled in.

The angel of God said to Daniel, "Fear not, Daniel: for from the first day that thou didst set thine heart to understand, and to chasten thyself

before thy God, thy words were heard, and I am
come for thy words. But the prince of the kingdom of Persia withstood me one and twenty days:
but, lo, Michael, one of the chief princes, came to
help me; and I remained there with the kings of
Persia. Now I am come to make thee understand
what shall befall thy people in the latter days: for
yet the vision is for many days." We see by this
Scripture (Dan. 10: 12-14) that God's angel was
stopped, hindered twenty-one days in getting the
answer to Daniel. Sometimes when one goes to
prayer he has not a spirit of prayer. There is no
liberty in prayer; there is no unction; things are
dry; things go slow; there is no oil; there is no
fire, and but little steam. But remember, always
remember, and never forget, we are to stay there,
keep at it, never let up until the fire falls.

Many times we have gone into prayer, and for
a half hour things looked gloomy, from the human
viewpoint. Why? The devil knew full well that
if he permitted us to pray through he would be
defeated. Hence, we felt sluggish, oftentimes
sleepy, and the devil would give us a good spell
of mind wandering. We could not collect our
thoughts, we could not concentrate our mind, but
we said, "We will stay here, we will keep at it, and
victory will come." Some good promises, a few

verses of a good song, looking back to how God has blessed, and answered prayer, will refresh one and often encourage the spirit of prayer.

A good wife in one of our revivals was impressed that that was the revival in which her husband must be saved. She asked this preacher to join her in fasting and prayer that God would pungently, miserably convict her husband. The meeting ran for several days; souls fell at the altar and swept through into the kingdom of grace. Her husband stood back, seemingly stubborn and hard to move. On Friday morning she was not at the breakfast table. I started to go into the parlor for a season of prayer. Opening the door we saw her kneeling by the davenport, engaged in earnest prayer. We went running up the stairway to our room, praising God. A deluge of grace swept through our soul, and we shouted aloud for some time. That morning, after preaching the sermon and making the altar call, the congregation standing, they had just sung two lines of the first stanza, when this husband fell full length, screaming, "Wife, come to me! God has got me down." That man was powerfully converted; shouted all that day. He lived just seven months, died in a halo of glory, and went sweeping through the pearly gates. This good wife felt led to pray much for him; she was impressed that this was the time for him to get saved; the Holy Ghost laid a heavy burden for his salvation upon her heart. The devil sent in a string of company, but this good woman would get away in earnest prayer by the hour. She knew when God led out in prayer she must follow; she knew when the Holy Ghost placed a crushing burden upon her heart she must not fail to wrestle in prayer. Suppose she had entertained her company and failed to wrestle in prayer; this husband might now be in Hell.

Let us be sure, when God leads us out in prayer, to go alone on our knees and wrestle and agonize until the victory comes. He will answer prayer. Yes, He answers prayer. Do not doubt it. Never doubt it. If He fails to answer to-day, it is because of some lesson to be taught. It is because there is a hindrance somewhere. When you pray clear through, the victory *will* come. It is *certain* to come. It has never failed to come. It paid Daniel to keep praying. It honored God for this man to hold on; it brought victory to the prayer life. We defeat God, rob Him of His glory, and thwart the pathway of the salvation of men, if we do not pray clear through. What a blessing it is to be counted worthy for God to place a burden of prayer upon one's heart.

CHAPTER XXI.

God Going Before.

Daniel 6: 10.

Daniel stands out in Christian history like the Rocky Mountains. He stands out a great Christian hero. He did mighty works for the Master. God crowned his life with much fruitfulness.

In answer to this earnest man's praying three times a day with his face toward Jerusalem, God did not answer by delivering this holy prophet from the den of lions. To have done this, God would have had to destroy the free moral agency of his enemies or place them in the casket. This He did not want to do, but God had a great lesson to teach Daniel's enemies. He wanted to show them that He not only had power to save this man from all sin, and keep him from actual, wilful sin; He not only had power to sanctify his soul, cleanse him from inbred sin, and empower him with the

Holy Ghost; had not only power to free him from
a man-fearing and a man-pleasing spirit, and
make him bold, courageous and fearless; had not
only power to make this man a great pray-er, a
great wrestler in agonizing prayer; had not only
power when this man's enemies placed the bloodhounds of Hell upon his track and meant to hound
him down, to give him sweet contentment and
blessed, quiet soul rest; had not only power to give
this man power over his enemies and audience
with the Triune God, and cause him, in the midst
of the sorest afflictions and the hardest tests of his
life to stand out quietly, serenely, and to have his
anchor hold fast; but, God also had power to precede this man to the den of lions, lock their
mouths, quench their thirst for human blood, and
put a quietness over them, until when Daniel was
lowered into the lions' den they walked about his
limbs as kittens would play about the ankle-joints
while you are building the fires of a winter morning.

God showed the world, and Daniel's greatest
enemies, that a sanctified man can be as safe in the
lions' den as in his room with his windows open
and his face toward Jerusalem, in the sweet,
blessed, enjoyable hour of prayer. Why? Because God meant to take care of Daniel in the

lions' den. Daniel was as much God's in the lions' den as in his own home. God had as much power to work miracles in the lions' den as He had in Daniel's own home. God has all power.

No doubt Daniel had a blessed, sweet night's rest. He may have prayed, meditated and rejoiced most all the night. He may have commanded one of the shaggy beasts to stretch himself upon the floor of the lions' den, and pillowing his head upon the same, slept soundly all night. No doubt Daniel had one of the sweetest nights of all his life. Next morning he was refreshed in body, mind and spirit. God covers us up in the hollow of His hand, and keeps us, preserves us, yea, fortresses us, in the riven side of His own Son. The angels of the Lord were encamped thick about Daniel that night. Be it understood and never forgotten, that when you are going through deep waters, long tunnels, sad afflictions, sore trials and darkness, and clouds are pressing down upon you hard, it is then that God is near. The Fourth Man was seen with the Hebrew children after they had gotten into the fiery furnace, and they only lost one thing in that fiery trial, and that was the strings the enemies had tied about their ankles and wrists. Fire purifies, burns up the dross, and makes us twenty-four carats pure gold.

This man Daniel had standing grace. He stood still. He stood quietly before God. He did not murmur. The waves ran high. The clouds were like midnight. The awful gales were blowing. The guns of the enemy were cracking. The bloodhounds of Hell were baying upon his track. Yet he was quiet. Why? Because he had the victory. Victory over the world. Victory over his enemies. Victory over environments. He had gotten this victory through protracted seasons of prayer. He prayed under the enemies' fire as he had been praying aforetime. He never put on one extra; he never did one thing that he had not been doing aforetime.

When loved ones get sick, badly sick, the doctors tell us that death is near, we get desperately in earnest; we fly to God; we fast; we pray; we wrestle in prayer; we stay up all night; we make vows and promises, "Yea, Lord, Thou shalt have a tenth. We will be honest, truthful with Thee. Spare the baby, the wife, or the husband, and we will go through with Thee at any cost"; but too often, and too soon, after the afflicted one has gotten well, someway, somehow, carelessness creeps in, and we are not as much in earnest six weeks afterwards as we were during the hours of severest pain.

Daniel prayed just as much when there were not sore afflictions and tests as he did when these things swept down upon his soul. He saw the hellish decree; he knew the devil had concocted this plan to defeat God's purposes: hence, he went to earnest prayer, and threw open his windows, and prayed with his face toward Jerusalem, as he had aforetime. Reader, will you mark the "aforetime"? Will you turn and read the sixth chapter of Daniel, and the tenth verse, carefully, upon your knees? Look at this man of God, and remember, *what God did for Daniel He will do for you, if you live as Daniel lived; if you do what Daniel did; if you will follow God as this man followed Him.* Daniel only stood the tests because of the fact that he had prayed clear through. His constant prayer life made him a conqueror, master of this devilish conspiracy, and Daniel was not only delivered, but God got glory through this man's soul travail.

Too many of us know too little about prayer, and sorry are we to confess that many do not want to be taught by the Holy Ghost how to pray. There is too much labor; too much self-denial. We do not like the idea of tearing ourselves away from our friends and staying with our face between our knees by the hour. The body does not enjoy this exercise. *We know so little about prayer because we pray so little* This old world, that is, the people in the world, would be 50 per cent. better if every Christian in Christendom had the real, vital spirit of prayer. We have the light. We talk about how God answered the prayers of the faithful patriarchs and prophets of by-gone days, but does not God need pray-ers to-day as much as He did in by-gone times? If He answered their prayers, and did such a tremendous work in the salvation of man and the defeating of the enemy, can He not do the same to-day, if we live upon our knees?

What is defeating God to-day, and robbing Jesus Christ of His glory? Prayerless lives. Oftentimes when preachers begin to get old, and have a barrel of sermons, they do not wrestle in prayer as they did when they were young and depended more upon God, seemingly. We mean this: old preachers should pray as much as young preachers; evangelists should pray as much in one meeting as in another. There is no such a thing as a burnt district. If we will pray clear through, God will work as long as there is one unsaved soul in a community. When Paul and Silas prayed clear through, the old jail took the Quaker shakes, and shook the shutters and doors from their

hinges and the stocks and chains from Paul's and
Silas' ankles and wrists, and they were liberated,
and a great revival broke out, and a church was
organized, with the Philippian jailer as first pastor. And if we will pray and wrestle as did Paul
and Silas, things will quake and shake in our community. It was said that when the disciples prayed
in a certain place, it was shaken. Oh, how the
world, the flesh and the devil hate prayer, oppose
prayer, and we are so negligent that we wait until
almost bedtime, when the body is tired, nerve
force running low, and the brain fagged—then we
go on our knees and not a few times, go to sleep,
and some of the family may have to wake us up.

The churches to-day are not the soul-saving
stations they should be; they are more of a nursery, more of a hospital. Why? Because of prayerless lives. So many go to church on Sabbath
morning, not from their knees, but from a Sunday
newspaper. They have no spirit of prayer. They
are not in a receptive attitude to be blessed or to
bless. They cannot get interested. They never
help the preacher. They go from the church as
they came—empty. But when men and women
get under the burden of prayer, get into the spirit
of prayer, get the real heart agony, soul travail,
then the six-foot-long icicle in the pulpit will melt.

the frost in the choir will melt, the snow in the pew will melt, altars will be crowded, bazaars will be a thing of the past, the kitchen department will be turned into a prayer room, and souls will be leaping into the kingdom of God.

Not long since, we were conducting a revival in a city church. The thing broke loose in the early part of the meeting. Bankers, lawyers, doctors and merchants ran to the altar with streaming eyes and wringing hands; they repented, confessed, and were beautifully saved. We said to the pastor, "What is the matter? There is a tremendous power upon this meeting." He took us across the city into the home of an afflicted woman. She had a big tumor in her stomach; was almost helpless. She grasped our hand and said, "Brother Harney, we've been praying two hours every day ever since the pastor announced you were to hold our revival, and I knew full well before the meeting began that God would give this good pastor and church and people a great sin-killing, soul-saving revival." She said, "I had prayed clear through. I had the witness that it was coming."

Another meeting was hard. The tide was against us. For nine days and nights we preached on Hell; one could almost see the blue flames and smell the sulphur. A sanctified man and his wife came to us and said, "Does your preaching have this effect everywhere you go? We can't shout a bit. We don't feel like it. In fact, we think you should change your line of preaching." But we were led by the Holy Ghost to keep at it; that is, keep preaching on Hell and sin. We urged the saints to pray. For nine days and nights there was not a break, but on Sunday the spirit of prayer swept in upon three or four saints, and they went down in real, vital soul travail; they prayed clear through.

On Monday morning we arose and took our text. We had preached about five minutes, when a very large, portly lady on our right, arose and said, "Brother Harney, I am in the way of this revival. Sister Smith and myself do not speak. We had a falling out two years ago and I feel that I am in the way of this revival, in the way of my family, in the way of my neighbors. I want to get out of the way. I purpose to get out of the way. I will meet Sister Smith half way, and we will bury the hatchet, handle and all." She started toward Sister Smith, and was knocked down by the power of God. A merchant arose and said, "I feel that I am in the way of this meeting. Mr. Brown, the merchant who runs the large department store, and myself are not on good terms; we speak, but there is a coolness, there is not the best feeling between us. I will meet Mr. Brown half way." With tears running down their faces they started toward each other, but both were knocked down by the power of God. We counted eleven prostrations that morning, and twenty-three were shouting at one time all over the church, and seventeen were saved in one service. Why? Because a few saints had banded themselves together to fast and pray until the fire fell. Like Mordecai and Esther, they had prayed three days and nights, and the Holy Ghost came and a great revival broke out and almost two hundred souls were saved. Why? Because these saints denied themselves of sleep and food, and felt that they must pray this meeting through.

God *will* answer prayer. He has *always* answered prayer. He may not answer right at the time; He may delay for His glory and our good, or, as the case may be, like it was in Daniel, tenth chapter, where the devil kept the angel of God with an answer to Daniel's prayer from getting to Daniel for twenty-one long days. But you keep praying; never let up; never let go. God *will* answer. He has always answered, for He is a prayer-hearing and a prayer-answering God. Dare to trust Him anywhere. *He will answer prayer.*

If you want to walk in the beautiful, victorious, shining pathway; if you want all the gates to fly open; if you want every block swept out of your way; if you want lions' mouths locked and fiery furnaces quenched, Red Seas to open up, Jordans to give you a dry pathway through, jails to shake off the doors and liberate you from prison—*pray clear through.* If you want a rich experience, a strong faith, and to do exploits for the Master—*pray clear through.* If you want to outride every storm of life, to go marching from ever battlefield with victory perched upon your banner—*pray clear through.* If you want the will of God concerning some work, some call, some plan about some friend—*pray clear through.* If you want the leadings of the Holy Ghost on any matter that pertains to His glory and your good—*pray clear through.* If you want an Isaac for a husband, a Rebekah for a wife—*pray clear through.* If you would have the Holy Ghost lubricate the wheels and belts of memory, unctionize your spirit for a fruitful service—*pray clear through.* If you would be more like Christ and less like the world—*pray clear through.* If you would be all like Christ, and none like the world—*pray clear through.* If you want to suit God,

please the Holy Ghost, and glorify Jesus Christ—
pray clear through. If you want His Word to
open up to you, and feed your soul, and make you
fat in grace—*pray clear through.* If you do not
want to go to Heaven empty-handed, or be a barren fig-tree—*pray clear through.*

You may not get the answer in an hour; you
may not get the answer in one day; you may not
get the answer in twenty days, but *keep at it.*
Never let up. If you have the burden of prayer,
and if the Spirit has led you out along any line in
the spirit of prayer, He will answer. *Keep at it.*
Pray clear through. God will never burden your
heart for anything, anybody, any work, or any
field, unless He will answer. God will not tease
you, and have you agonize for something that cannot be obtained. He has said, "Blessed are they
which do hunger and thirst after righteousness:
for they *SHALL* be *filled.*"

The reason why so many people have no burden of prayer is, they have no spiritual life. Where
there is natural life there must be an appetite, and
where there is spiritual life, necessarily, there
must be a desire for prayer, a hunger to get alone
with God. A dead man does not want anything
to eat. He has no appetite. A sinner, a backslidden man, has no desire for prayer; there are no

leadings to the prayer life. But every child of
God who is living close to God, hungers for the
prayer life. He enjoys praying. He lingers upon
his knees long and often. The more we pray, the
more we want to pray. The more we pray, the
more we feel like praying. The more we pray, the
longer we will pray, and the less we tire in prayer.
The more we pray, the stronger will be the prayer
life, for it is by earnest, protracted prayer that we
grow in grace in the prayer life. The more we
pray, the greater the appetite for prayer will be.
The more we pray, the more we will plan to get to
pray. The more we pray, the more we will see
strength, courage, and growth in faith coming to
us through much prayer.

If we want to win a Sunday-school class to
God; if we want to win some neighbor to Jesus
Christ; if we want access to carry a message of
salvation, let us go from our knees. God will
open the door when you get qualified. How
sweet, how delightful, how restful, to linger in
His presence by the hour in prayer. Oftentimes
when we have been gone in revival work for six
weeks, and reach our home, that sweet wife who
has stood by the stuff and taken care of the babies
while we have been gone those long weeks, is so
glad to see us coming, and we are so glad to look

into her gray eyes, that not a few times we sit
and talk, talk, talk, until late, yea, deep into the
night. We enjoy talking to our wife, for she is
the mother of our sweet babies. We enjoy talking
to our wife, for God gave her to us. Ah! you tell
me when you get married to Jesus Christ that you
cannot enjoy hours at His feet. Something is
radically wrong when the wife does not enjoy the
husband's company. There is something in the
way. So it is with a Christian when he does not
enjoy much prayer, protracted seasons of prayer,
something must be radically wrong. Something
is in the way. He must have been flirting with old
Splitfoot.

If you want the burning witness in your heart,
the fire to burn in your soul, the Blood to cleanse
you—*pray clear through*. Let us pray as never
before for a great revival to rush in upon this
generation. Let us earnestly pray Jesus Christ to
send a withering, blistering conviction upon sinners, and salvation to earnest penitents. Let us
live on our knees. *God will answer.*

CHAPTER XXII.

Great Revival in Answer to Prayer.

It was one of the best seasons in the whole year for a revival, late in the fall, yet warm and with a full moon.

Pastor Baird called Will Selby and myself to hold a series of evangelistic meetings in his church at Tabor, Ky. At first the crowds were very small, but we began praying and calling on God and fasting every other morning. Some of the saints prayed also; many of them were to be found on their knees in the early hours of the morning praying earnestly. In answer to our united prayers, conviction, deep, pungent conviction, settled upon the unsaved and they began coming out to the meetings.

There was a widow in that community who did not believe in the altar nor heart-felt religion. Her daughter, a girl of sixteen summers, got under deep conviction for sin and one day came to

us and said, "Oh, Brother Harney, if mother were
not in my way, I would rush to the altar, but mother says if I go there she will disown me." We
asked publicly how many would join us in fasting
the next morning and in praying thirty minutes
to God to let deep conviction fall on the mother's
heart; three responded. The next night we again
called for volunteers and three more joined us.
As I walked out of the church after service, I said
to the mother, "God will make you so miserable
that you cannot sleep or eat; the Holy Spirit is
on your track, the saints are wrestling in prayer
for you, and you had better yield to God. It is
dangerous to resist the Holy Spirit, to refuse to
walk in so much light." She left the church at
once, replying, "God will never answer such prayers."

The next night we again called for those who
would pray for this sister, and three or four more
united with us, and the next morning as we walked into the church the daughter came running,
saying, "Oh, Brother Harney, mother is the most
miserable being on earth, slept but very little last
night. After we went home she said, 'They think
that God can keep me from eating, but I will show
them.' She made some coffee and got several little
cakes and sat down to the table to eat this lunch,

when immediately she had a deep impression that
should she touch a thing or drink a drop of coffee
she would be paralyzed, and then she broke down
and wept bitterly and confessed that God was answering prayer."

After the daughter had told me this, and as I
went down the church aisle, I noticed the mother
in one of the pews, but instead of the fine hat she
had been wearing she had on a sunbonnet and her
eyes were red with weeping. She looked at me and
said, "You are responsible for this misery, you
are responsible if I starve to death," and we looked
into her face and saw that her heart was broken
before God. I answered, "If you do not yield, if
you refuse to listen to the Holy Spirit, His earnest pleadings with your heart, I fear you will soon
die." She cried out in alarm, "Oh! don't pray
God to kill me." We answered, "We will not do
that, but you must yield to God."

She arose from where she was sitting, came
forward and took one of the front seats, and at
the close of the earnest message that God laid on
our hearts, did not walk to the altar, she could not,
but knelt right where she was and screamed out at
the top of her voice, "My God, have mercy on me!
My God, have mercy on me! Can'st Thou forgive
me? Is there any redemption for me? Has the

Holy Ghost forsaken me? Have I sinned away my day of grace? Is there any hope?" She became desperate, she prayed, promised and confessed, and soon the regenerating power of God came flooding her soul and she leaped, and shouted the praises of God.

Taking us by the hand, she weepingly testified, "How I thank God for this Christian people! Had it not been for the prayers of the saints, I would have been lost. I thought that I was right, but I awakened to the sad fact that I was only a member of the church and not a child of Jesus Christ, but now, thank God! there is a clear, burning, definite witness in my soul that I am His and He is mine. I know it and feel it, my burden has rolled away. Jesus has come and there is heavenly sunlight in my soul. Oh, everything looks so beautiful, so lovely, and I am so happy. This is what I have needed all these years. Now I can be a help and guide to my daughter. Thank God for the old-time revival, for a revival that has revived me, that has brought peace and light into our community, into our church, into our home! Now we can have family prayers, study the Word of God, say grace at the table, and have a little heaven here to go to Heaven from."

Christian worker, we have given this illustration of the power of God to answer prayer, that your faith may be encouraged. You go to a place to hold a meeting, the crowds are small and seemingly circumstances and surroundings are against you, but go quietly in earnest, secret prayer before God, get the saints to unite with you, and fast and pray until He answers, for He will answer. He can break down stubborn wills, He can break through indifference, He can bring deep, heart-burning conviction to the unsaved, He can make men and women to so feel the need of Jesus Christ as their Savior that they will be glad, they will plead for a chance, to find the mercy-seat. Let us not say a district is "burnt over." It may be that the lack of a revival is because we have not taken hold of the throne of God; we have not carried the burden of souls of the people for whom we are to labor. Mighty God, put on us our responsibility, help us to see that we shall meet again these men and women to whom we ministered, before the great white throne of the Judge of all the earth.

Can we then say that our skirts are clean from the blood of all men? I have never yet gone to God in agony of prayer for a soul; I have never felt a crushing, immutable burden over a soul's condition before God, but what God put on me such a prayer, a constant prayer, that I could only

weep and hold on to Him until He gave the witness that the answer was coming. Oh, pray, pray
on, pray clear through. The God of Heaven will
answer. He has never failed. His promise is
unbreakable. His Word is immutable. You can
claim the victory, and the Captain of your salvation, in answer to believing prayer, will give it.

CHAPTER XXIII.

Paul and Silas Praying Clear Through.

These holy men of God were conducting a soul-saving, sin-killing, devil-driving revival in Philippi. On their way to the place of worship, Paul proposed a street service. They mounted a box and began to sing the sweet songs of Zion and the crowds thronged about them. Soon Silas led in prayer that melted many hearts and caused tears to flow freely, then Paul, the mighty preacher of the Word, opened the Gospel that pricked hearts, uncovering sin, showing men that restitution and confession must be made, before God would pardon.

By the time Paul closed this heart-rending message, a talented actress came screaming through the crowds, falling at the mourner's bench, crying, "Men and brethren, what must I do to be saved?" Paul and Silas said, "Confess, repent, and keep on until you strike rock bottom."

She cried, "I can't."   Silas said, "This is the only
way, no card-signing will bring a know-so, heart-
felt case of religion.   You must not only give up
your sins, and go out of the sin business, but you
must repent of what you have done.   Suppose we
should go in debt sixty dollars worth at the store,
and then come again in a few weeks, purchasing
another sixty dollars worth, and saying to the
merchant, 'I purpose never to go in debt again,
I will pay as I go from this on.'   The merchant
would say, 'That is good, but what about the
sixty dollars you owe me?' "

The actress followed this godly instruction.
struck rock bottom, the fire flew, grace filled her
heart, and the Holy Ghost witnessed that all her
sins were forgiven.   She, leaping up, stood and
began shouting and praising God.   Her face was
wreathed in heavenly sunlight.

One who had seen all this ran to the theater
men, saying, "There will be no theater to-night,
no play."   The manager said, "Yes indeed, we
have one of the finest, one of the most talented
women of the entire country, who will act to-
night."   "Yes, but," said the man, "I tell you she
will not act to-night, I know what I am talking
about."   The manager looked at him and said,
"Are you crazy?"   "No, but I tell you, sir, as I

was coming to the theater, I heard some sweet singing on a street corner, and went across and there on a goods' box, two men, with bright, shining countenances, were preaching the Gospel; some were in tears, others wringing their hands, while your actress, who had elbowed her way through the crowd, was standing near the box shaking from head to foot. At the close of the sermon, she fell at the goods' box crying for mercy. Soon the preachers were down by her side, exhorting her to quit sin, and make her crooked paths straight. Soon she jumped to her feet, and I tell you we had some shouting." The manager says, "You don't say so. A talented woman, one who had signed a contract to play so many nights, an actress of her ability, attending a street service, and getting so excited that she would permit herself to make such demonstrations on the street? I can't believe it, it can't be so, you are wholly mistaken." "Well," said the man, "come with me."

The two hurried off up the street, and as they came near the box meeting, Silas was assisting the actress upon the goods' box, so she could give her experience. She began by saying, "As I came along the street, I heard the song that my darling mother often sang to us children. It

brought up those happy by-gone days. Mother
stood before me saying, 'My child, my child, stop
at this service.' I found myself with others, listening to the songs and sermon; somewhere, I
caught a glimpse of my poor lost soul and ah!
such awful agony took hold upon me that I began
to shake all over. I tried hard to control myself;
I said, 'This will never do, am I losing my mind?'
but shake I would. When Brother Paul gave the
invitation, I was glad to go down there by other
poor lost sinners, just like other poor lost sinners.
I confessed all my sins. The devil said, 'What
about the contract?' I said, 'I am done now and
forever hereafter with theaters, plays, all that is
wrong.' I told the Lord if He would pardon my
sins, I would be anything for Him. I had much
to give up, to repent of, but when I did all they
told me and all God showed me, the fire fell, the
glory rolled into my soul and I tell you, I know
from head to foot now that Jesus saves me.
Glory! My soul is happy. Let me exhort you all
to do likewise and let this day sweet knowledge
of sins forgiven come to you."

The manager saw for himself that that night's
play, so far as that actress was concerned, was
done for. He went to the head men and said that
something must be done here and now, to stop

this religion. "It is spreading, it is breaking into our business," said he, "and causing folks to make fools of themselves, by confessing their sins, and restoring money that they had gotten by burning things to get the insurance, and in other fraudulent ways. You know if this strikes us, we are ruined, for some of us have never gotten an honest dollar. Such a religion would bankrupt us, and I fear some of us would land in the penitentiary. We should not allow such evangelists and such a Gospel to get into our church, and I am rejoicing that they are largely being kept out and crowded to brush arbors and tent-meetings. We must call for a level-headed, brainy, safe, conservative man, who will preach us a sermonette twice on Sunday, while we attend theaters, have our card parties and dances, go to the circus and skating rinks, and drink our wines, but be it understood, we must pay big and bring up all the collections, we must organize different societies and work like Trojans."

This speech excited and influenced the minds of the leaders; they rushed off to the street meeting, and arrested Paul and Silas. Paul said, "Why arrest peaceful citizens? We are preaching the old-time Gospel that brings old-time results." But they hurried them to the court, had a mock trial, and sentenced them to a whipping and the dungeon cell. The dungeon was cold and damp, not one ray of light to be seen. With their ankles and wrists in stocks and bands, and with bleeding backs, they were left alone to suffer thirst and hunger.

Toward midnight, after meditation and secret prayer, Paul said, "Silas, lead us in prayer." Silas prayed, "Our Father who art in Heaven, hallowed be Thy name, Thy kingdom come, Thy will be done. Teach us to pray. Thou seest our bleeding backs, Thou knowest our sufferings, hear us while we pray. We know that Thou art almighty. Thou didst open the Red Sea, Thou didst open up the Jordan, Thou didst tear down the walls of Jericho, Thou didst stop the moon and the sun, Thou didst lock lions' mouths, and quench fiery furnaces, Thou art God." Paul began to shout, and said, "Pray, Silas, I feel the power." Silas prayed, "Through one man's prayers Thou didst lock up the skies, through three hundred Thou didst give the devil a galling defeat, yea, Thou didst blow Thy breath in the mulberry-trees and put to flight all the devils upon a battlefield." By this time Paul was shaken by the power, he began to praise God, the stocks and bands fell from his ankles and wrists, and he leaped around the dungeon shouting, "Silas, my soul is on fire."

Then there was a tremendous concussion, such a shaking as they had never felt before. Silas, too, had been freed from his chains, and he was making the welkin ring. The old jail was shaking, reeling, staggering like a drunken man, jail doors and windows were crashing, and prisoners were leaping from their beds of slumber, thinking the world was coming to an end. The jailer, being thrown from his bed by this earthquake, screamed to his wife, "What is the matter? What has taken place?" Looking toward the prison, he saw things luminous as at midday, and tremblingly said, "I'll kill myself, all the prisoners have escaped." Grabbing his sword, he was about to commit suicide, when Paul cried out, "Mr. Jailer, kill not thyself, for we are all in here, there isn't a 'Come-outer' in the crowd." The jailer cried out, "What must I do to be saved?" He fell at the mourner's bench and, by daylight, he and his household were converted, a church organized, and he was pastor of the church at Philippi.

CHAPTER XXIV.

A MULTI-MILLIONAIRE SAVED AND SALOONS PUT OUT OF BUSINESS THROUGH PRAYER.

In the Southland, where flowers always bloom, the mocking-bird warbles its notes of melody all the day long, and the darkies hum their old-time melodies in the cotton patches, making merry the passer-by, in that land once lived a poor family. This family had an afflicted daughter, who was minus a left arm and a left limb and whose right hand had only two fingers and a thumb. Her right limb was so drawn and twisted that she was wholly unable to walk; she was bed-ridden in an upstairs room, the floor of which was carpetless and on the walls not a single picture; a rickety old bed and one stool were the furniture. Upon this bed lay this afflicted child for fifteen years.

One day a Salvation Army lassie found this humble home and in conversation with the mother, learned about the sadly afflicted child. She was taken by the mother to the child's bedside and there, in her Christlike manner, told the sweet story of Jesus in sweetest, simplest language. The child, who had been taught by her mother until she was a good reader, became much interested. This Salvation Army girl kept going to the home daily, taking good religious papers, books, and tracts. The child read and got hungry for Jesus.

One night she dreamed that, if she were to give her heart to Christ, He would make her a useful channel to lead multitudes to Him. She wondered how this could be true. She said, "Here I am with this horrible affliction, born this way, what can I do? I have but little education, unable to go to school, my father a day laborer and so poor that he cannot do anything for me, so the dream can never come true."

But one night when we were all soundly asleep, she began seeking God in earnest. She cried out, "Oh, Lord, I have but two fingers and a thumb, and if you will save me they shall work always for Thee. Forgive my sins. I am so sorry that I have so neglected Thee, I will, I can, I do believe that Jesus here and now saves me." The clock in the tower was striking twelve, the stars and moon now shone brightly, but the light that broke into that soul at that midnight hour was much brighter than the sun at noonday. She could not help it, in fact she did not try; the laughter, the hallelujahs and praises rang out upon the night air until the whole family were aroused from their slumbers and came into her room, and they soon saw that she had been with Jesus.

The Spirit there and then began a great work through her feeble instrumentality; her father was gloriously reclaimed by her bedside that night, and her brother and sister were saved; it was a great night for the family. The next morning, calling her father and mother into her room, she told them how the Spirit had been whispering that there was a work for her to do. The parents encouraged her, the mother took the girl in her arms, saying, "Papa and Mamma will do their best to help you."

The next day she said to her father, "Papa, bring me a lead pencil and a tablet for I am to preach my first sermon at one o'clock this afternoon." The pencil and tablet were purchased and brought to her room. She had spent the forenoon in quiet, earnest prayer, that Jesus would bless her first effort, and the Spirit gave her her first message. He had impressed her that she must write across one page, "Where will you

spend Eternity?" She wrote this simple line, then
cried from the depths of her heart, "O thou
blessed Spirit, let this paper strike the right party
squarely in the face." She prayed more earnestly, she got a real burden, she felt that God had
heard and would answer her heart-cries. She
watched the clock and prayed, resting her faith
upon this promise, "Ask, and ye shall receive."
She read and re-read this promise and again she
would pour out her earnest soul to God in prayer,
saying, "Now, Father, send the right party along.
It is only five minutes until time to preach my first
sermon. The sermon is ready, and so am I.
hurry the right party, right under my window."

Just then the clock struck one, so, taking the
slip of paper, she held her hand out of the window
and cried, "O Lord, please let this strike the right
man or the right woman squarely in the face.
Use it to bring awful conviction; use it to show
the right one his lost and undone condition; use
it to bring some one to Jesus. You shall have all
the glory. You shall get all the praise. This poor
deformed child does not want one bit."

The paper slipped out of her hand and was
winged by a kind zephyr into the face of a great
banker. He grabbed the paper as it came across
both eyes and behold, "Where will you spend

Eternity?" struck him like a cannon ball. He
staggered, he was dazed, he was alarmed, he was
frightened, he looked up, he looked around, he
said, "I am going to die soon, this is a warning.
God sent this by some angel. I must get ready.
I am an awful sinner. I have neglected God for
business. I have made piles of money, but I am
a lost man; I have laid up treasures on earth and
I have not any bank stock in Heaven." Soon he
was wringing his hands, crying aloud, "I am
lost."

The girl's mother heard the pitiful cries of
this rich man and hurried to him, saying, "What
is the matter? Are you sick? Do you want me
to call a doctor? Where do you live? Must I
call the bus?" "Woman, read this." As soon as
the mother saw the slip of paper and the handwriting, she knew what it meant, she saw that
God had honored, blessed, and used her child to
break the heart of this great business man. She
said, "That slip of paper came from yonder window. My deformed child wrote that. She has
been converted, and feels that God has called her
to do a great work." This man, with tear-filled
eyes and a bleeding heart, said, "Take me to her
room."

On entering her room, the banker said, "Oh,

child, how came you to throw that paper out just
at that moment? How came you to write just
that line? It has broken my heart. It has shown
me my awful condition. I am rich in money,
but a pauper in religion. I would rather have
this old bed, this old stool, this carpetless room,
and have what you now enjoy, than all my wealth.
I am a miserable man, and with this poverty, you
are a beautiful, happy Christian girl. You look
so happy; now, as I kneel by your bedside, place
that hand that wrote that line, upon my head and
pray Him who carried that paper into my face,
to have mercy on me and to save me, for I am
willing to do anything possible to get what you
have."

He knelt, the hand rested upon his head, and
such a prayer could only come from a heart filled
with the fullness of God. How tenderly she
prayed, how sympathetic she was in her prayer
She simply poured out her whole soul in earnest
prayer. Here was her first fruit, here was the result of her first message; she saw at a glance that
her dream was coming true.

The Lord got a deeper grip upon that man's
conscience. What confessions! what deep repentance! He began to pray, and the more he
prayed, the louder he prayed. Soon, with stream-

ing eyes, he had this girl in his arms shouting, "God has forgiven me. Oh, I am so happy! We are childless at our home, not because we plan or want to be childless, I want a child, I have been hungry for some child to call me father, and why can't I adopt you? Then I could get you a nice rubber-tired chair, hire a strong woman to roll your chair, and you could go about all day, preaching, working for the Master and come in home at night. Then I could fix a small box to your chair and you could carry tracts, papers, and Bibles." The child said, "That would be nice, my papa is too poor to buy me a chair. We will pray about it, and if our Lord leads, I am willing to be your child."

That night the whole story was told to her father, they prayed together, God led, and through this seemingly strange Providence, the child was adopted into the banker's family. Soon she was seen on the streets in her new rubber-tired chair, preaching the glad story of redemption. The banker and his wife were simply overjoyed. How grateful they were that God had given them a daughter.

This child saw for the first time in her life the awful destruction of the liquor traffic. She was amazed to see men staggering, falling, spending their money for that which brought misery, when their families at home needed bread and meat, clothes and fuel. A burden for the destruction of these murder mills (the saloons) came rushing upon her. That night her banker-father told her of the murderers, criminals, and thieves; how the penitentiaries are crowded, and over one hundred thousand going to a drunkard's grave and a drunkard's hell annually. The child sobbed and cried all night, she saw strong men, noble men, fathers and sons, husbands and brothers, by the thousands, being slaughtered by these hellish monsters. Soon she began to lecture upon the streets; she would go into the saloons and pray and beg men to not sell that which destroyed home, character, and honor.

One saloon-keeper got so miserable that he could not stay in the business; he seemingly saw himself at the Judgment, and behold women and children gnashed upon him, shaking their bony fingers in his face, saying, "You took the carpet from our home, you took the clothes from the wardrobe, you took the eatables from the pantry, you sold our house over our heads, you put us out on the cold streets, your business destroyed our husband and father, you made him kill his neighbor, and then the law that gave you the license to sell the damnable stuff, took our father and hanged him. Oh! such a law, such a constitution, to license a thing that destroys her citizenship. Citizens should be protected, but the law that should protect turns loose upon innocent people, and while many object, these destructive, heartless murder mills, these hellish saloons, care not for our boys, they must be fed. What is the raw material? Young men, noble sons, who would make honorable citizens, if it were not for these hell holes. Woolen-mills turns out cloths to protect us from the winter, wheatmills turns out flour to feed us and make us stronger. These mills are an honor to any community, to any citizenship; they are legitimate, they are necessary, but these mills of hell destroy, corrupt, debauch, degrade, disgrace, they sow harlotry, crime, vice, immorality, and wholly unfit man for his best interest."

The next morning at the breakfast table, this godly child told her father and mother how God had so burdened her that she had not slept a wink all night, and now, she had a new field of labor. She was called to put the saloons out of business and purposed, by God's grace and their assistance, to wage a relentless war upon these man-destroyers. Her parents promised their assistance. That day was spent in silent prayer all alone in her room, and she received this promise, Proverbs 2: 10-12. She laughed, she cried, she shouted. Her mother, hearing her, ran upstairs saying, "Have you prayed through?" The child said, "Yes, glory to God! The saloons will go. I have the victory."

The next day she began her holy war, she bombarded nine saloons, she kept it up, she scattered good temperance literature. The saloon-keeper who had gotten under such awful conviction, went to another saloon-keeper and said, "Bob, let's quit the dirty business. Our boys will soon be old enough to drink." He had never thought of other mothers' sons. The two men agreed to quit, then joined the girl in her battle against this awful enemy of sobriety, virtue, truthfulness, upright character, and noble manhood and womanhood. She got one of the best temperance lecturers to come for a ten-days campaign. This drew great crowds, and soon three other saloons closed. By this time, the mayor and town council read clearly the handwriting on the wall and saw their doom, unless they refused to re-license these devilish, destructive murder mills, and so the others had to close.

This child one day read about an evangelist

who was having a sweeping revival in another
town. She urged her father and they went over
to the meeting. They soon saw that this was the
Lord's work, and made a date with the evangelist and his singer. The five churches joined in
this great work. Old and young said they never
had seen such interest manifested in religious
work in that town. People came by the hundreds,
by dark the great building was packed. A great
religious awakening broke out and a tremendous
soul-saving revival followed. Hundreds were led
to Christ. One of the pastors said to the banker,
"Your child, by her earnest prayers and faithful
work, has brought about this great change. It
is wonderful, simply marvelous to see men who
once sold whiskey now working in this meeting,
and the drunkards, the gamblers are being saved
as well as the upper classes."

One night after going home from this great
revival, while meditating, she saw how her dream
was coming true, how God had worked, how
God had multiplied her usefulness, what a marvelous fruitage He had given although she was
poor and deformed. Christians, wake up, listen!
give what you have to God, consecrate your all
upon the altar, present your bodies a living sacrifice for He is using all who are at all useable.

If you are not being used, whose fault is it?
Jesus delights to use all, no matter what your de-
formity, your physical infirmities, your inabilities,
just give Him a chance. He will put all the imps
to flight who chuckle and whisper, "There is no
use in trying." Let us to-day, let us this hour,
let us this minute, consecrate our all to Him.
"O Lord, help us, look down upon us in pity.
Thou knowest us, our weakness is too great unless Thou help us. What can we do without
Thee? It makes us hide our face in shame when
we see how Thou didst so marvelously use this
poor afflicted child. Help those of us who have
strong bodies to consecrate our every power to
Thee. We will do it, Thou mayest count on us.
We thank Thee for thy goodness, for Thy patience, for Thy forgiveness, for Thy forgetful-
ness of our many sins, and we promise Thee a
better service. We are Thine, soul, spirit and
body, to go, to stay, or to send. Count on us,
Lord. Amen!

CHAPTER XXV.

THE BEGINNING OF A GREAT REVIVAL.

The church was cold, in a lukewarm state; most of the members were dead; seemingly all that was needed was a funeral. A small crowd greeted us for the first week. There was no enthusiasm and not enough religious force to send the hand around the dial plate. It was hard preaching and harder praying. There was ice in the pew, frost in the choir, and zero weather everywhere. The religious grass was frightfully short and the folks were so poor, so weak, that we could pull no load. The clouds were dark and hung very low, a dense fog hung all over the town. Some said, "You might just as well quite, there isn't anything doing and there is no likelihood of there being a stir. First, because the enemy, hoof, hide, and horns, has had this city for a lifetime, and he is so entrenched, so fortified that it's impossible to man any heavy artillery against him, or to force him out of his fortified positions. Second, the folks who profess live like the folks who never did follow Jesus   Nothing comes to town that you do not see a big bunch of church folks in the lead.   You will find scores of them in a circus, dozens at progressive euchre parties, and Sunday baseball parks are filled with those whom you will see, on communion Sunday, acting like saints."   So all seemed to prophesy that there could be nothing done that would as much as look like a revival.

One night there was a high "nor'-wester," whose bleak winds spelled out loudly twenty degrees below zero and an eight-inch snow.   Our crowd was smaller than ever, and the enthusiasm, if we had had any, was frozen up.   We could almost see and hear imps chuckling in every direction, and whispering, "You might just as well close.   This hard preaching, this going out into zero weather, is more than likely to bring on pneumonia; you have been sneezing and coughing to-day, and your chest is getting tight.   Aren't you aware of the fact that man is a free moral agent?   Didn't God try to keep Adam and Eve from that bad, puckering fruit?   But they went right on, across light, and people's mouths are still puckering because of their eating that fruit,

their abuse of free moral agency. These people
are free beings, have heads of their own, and you
can never bring them over from their pre-con-
ceived ideas. Bigger men, brighter men, greater
men, greater preachers than you have been here
by the week, and have shelled the woods with
heavy artillery until it looked like the stars would
melt from their golden sockets, the moon would
weep herself to death, and the mighty king of
day would hide his face in shame all because these
giants, with their tremendous logic could not
break through the strong walls of stubbornness."

Again they would say, "You are foolish. You
are a young man, there is too bright a future before you for you to wear your life away, injure
your body, and give yourself preacher's sore
throat, trying to win these people who have sinned
away their day of grace." And again, "You have
been here one week; you have fasted almost every
morning and prayed two and three hours each
day, and there isn't one bit of interest. The pastor, although a good man, and a brilliant fellow,
has not said one encouraging word to you, but,
both by looks and acts, shows how hopeless the
undertaking."

Then Satan came along and said, "If the
church folks are so wholly indifferent, would

rather go to a nickleodeon than come to a revival, would it not be best for you to go where
you will be appreciated and where the folks will
be interested? I feel sorry for you. This people
does not want the Gospel, they will not receive it;
you can lead a horse to water, but you can not
make him drink. Russell has proven that there
isn't any Hell, and that's a dead doctrine, therefore this people resent and reject such a back-
woods, Dark Ages Gospel; now, if you were to
lecture on 'A Trip from the North Star to the
Moon,' you might attract the people. Or if on
'The Cyclones Sweeping Across the Face of the
Sun,' you would have a packed house.

"Why not get the crowds? Why not use
means to that end? There are men in mission
halls, under small tents and brush arbors, preaching to a handful, who could just as easily be
preaching in the centers of population to thousands, if they would only listen to me and change
their tactics and preach a twentieth-century gospel. We are all aware of the fact that this is a
progressive age, and, to keep pace, we must necessarily be a progressive people, hence, the things
used a century ago can never be in use to-day.
Washington rode in a stage coach to Washington, D. C.; President Wilson went in a flying

palace car. Your forefathers plowed with wood-
en plows fastened to an ox; to-day you have
great steam plows. So the Gospel which, a century ago, attracted the masses and turned the
multitudes Gospelward, to-day, with the scientific
investigation, the great libraries, the mighty
brain girth of so many, will have to be made to
suit the times.

"You will have to make a radical change in
your manner and method of conducting these
evangelistic campaigns, and you will have to
change the matter of your sermons, for culture is
the great demand of this day and time. The more
science you can pack into your messages, the
greater your sweeps of rhetoric, and the more
powerful your logic and oratory, the greater
preacher you will be considered and the larger
will be your salary.

"I have had this little chat with you purposely, for I admire your zeal and pluck, and have
thus advised that you may have great success
in your efforts among this wealthy, up-to-date,
wide-awake cultured people. If you ever win
them you will always have them. They are not
soft, easily moved by deathbed scenes and grave-
yard tales. They are a people not given to much
weeping or emotionalism. Now, before leaving

you, let me urge you to be a constant student of
Hindu philosophy, and to use philosophical terms.
By so doing, your crowds will think that they
have a master in the pulpit. Preach more to the
heads, for there is but little heart in anything
these days. Let me further advise that you copy
after great men, get their manners, cute phrases,
pert sayings, and you will soon make a reputation. Let no old fogy instil into your head to be
original, for there is no originality to-day.

"Again, do not be too hard on the people; do
not expect too much of them, for they are weaklings. Remember that you can get hundreds to
sign a card and the papers will blow you all over
pressdom, and most people will think that you
are having a sweeping revival. This way you
will not have to wear your life out so soon, you
will not have to preach so hard, and then you will
not have to fast and go hungry, and wrestle and
agonize hours in prayer. This card-signing way
is so restful for you and easy for the people.
They do not have to confess, dig down, repent,
restore; then the rich will take to you; folks who
have been a little crooked in business will flock
to you like bees to a hive. The Gospel of repentance is a hard Gospel. For instance, here is
a man with a fine business, a lovely home, a big

auto; getting along nicely, until one of these cranks who everlastingly preaches on confession comes to town. This rich man gets under his sway, his hypnotic influence, and confesses that he got most of his money in a swindling way, so looses his fine home and flourishing business—all because this crank hammered on the Gospel of repentance. It would have been much better for him, had he had a cultured mind, a classical education and preached a beautiful, soothing gospel. This rich man would have contributed $1,000.00, but he got only $140.00 and wrecked a good business. Many say he did not only ruin the business of this man but caused the man to turn preacher, and that spells for his family, a scant living and little hope of ever having a permanent dwelling-place. It is very discouraging, for look at this man six weeks ago—great throngs of customers, a mansion, proud family, hundreds of friends, and to-day in a rented shack, conducting meetings in a mission hall. He tells folks that the Lord convicted him, gave him light, and by walking in that light, he had to make wrongs right, black white, and, in so doing, has plunged his family into poverty.

"Let me advise you once more, before leaving, rearrange all your sermons, make them more

cultured, take up-to-date topics, follow such lights
as the great Dr. Blank. He sneers at Hell and
the Virgin birth of Christ, but my! he holds down
the biggest thing in Christendom, and gets a big
pile of gold to boot. He lectures between spells
all over the country, is in great demand. The
Chautauquas are crazy for him.

"You can climb, for I have given you enough
counsel to take you to the top rung, to give you
an international reputation, to pile thousands of
gold into your coffers. You would be a fool to
go on and preach to handfuls and get a meager
compensation, keeping your family on scanty
fare. Let me urge you, as your best friend, to
climb, there is plenty of room at the top, but the
bottom is always crowded. Your family can
easily ride in fine autos, live in a mansion, go in
the best walks of society, have a wardrobe packed
with clothing, a pantry filled with plenty, all be
in ease and comfort, and you a great leader, if
you will only follow this friendly advice. There
is no excuse for you, as you have had too good
opportunities and too good scholastic training
to go ahead in the same old rut and keep your
family on starvation rations. Can't you see in
the not distant future that glittering high steeple?
can't you hear the great rolling pipe organ, and

that high-sounding choir? Now, make your choice; be somebody, be a coming man, be in great demand, command a pile of gold, and ease and comfort will crown your old days and your stomach will never go empty."

The second week had come and everything was as bad as ever. We never saw things freeze tighter; there was no warmth at all. Some of our best people had become so discouraged that they advised pulling stakes, and it seemed to us, from the human viewpoint, that a revival was far, far away.

About this time God sent a Mordecai into the camp; he was a clerk in a drygoods store. He came to us saying, "I have to work hard all day, can't get here only of a night, and have but little time to pray through the day. I will do this, I'll meet you here in the church at 3 A. M. and we will pray until 6, and will keep this up until we see the cloud the size of a man's hand. God says where two or three pray, in His name, He will be with them. Now let us agree, and pray until He breaks up this stubborn indifference. Mordecai and Esther prayed three days and nights and God saved the Jewish people. Is He not still the same God? Will He not answer us as He did

Mordecai and Esther, and as He answered Daniel?"

I said, "I will go into this covenant with you with this understanding, if you get to the church first, ring the bell until I get there, and if I beat you there, I will be pulling on the rope when you reach the church."

At 2: 30 A. M. I awoke, hurried my toilet and had reached the high-school building when Brother V—— began ringing the church bell. In a few minutes lights were in every home, and men running through the yards, dressing, and screaming, "Fire! fire! fire!" We yelled, "Yes, at the church." Soon that big church had 320 souls in it. Think of it, at three o'clock in the morning, and zero weather, too, and a zero congregation! How that good man did shout as he saw the people flocking into the church at that early morning hour.

God saw that we meant business, that we were determined, that our hearts were breaking under the tremendous, crushing burden; He saw that two of us had agreed, and answered before we had time to pray. There was much excitement and people from various walks of life crowded into the church. We took our text and preached in the power and demonstration of the Holy

Spirit, and conviction deep and pungent fell on that crowd. People sobbed aloud; the State's attorney jumped from his seat and hurried to the altar. What confessions! how he cried to God for mercy, for forgiveness. He promised there at the altar to burn up an Ingersol library and there and then he and his wife found pardon.

There was a going in the mulberry-trees, and the meeting ran at high tide until Sunday morning. That morning while I was preaching the power fell and the head of the First National Bank, like a hoop came rolling by me down out of the choir into the aisle, screaming, "My God! I am a lost man." There seemingly was a shock, a great break, and eighty-three rushed to the altar. Such a scene as followed is indescribable; about fifty men were gloriously converted that morning. Such shouting, such rejoicing, could only follow such an altar service; children were in the arms of their parents, parents were in the arms of their children. One old sainted man attending this meeting from another town said to me, "I have never seen such a scene, this is simply out of the ordinary. God is here, God is with us." In this meeting over three hundred were saved, and scores joined the church.

It pays to be prayerful, and never listen to the

whisperings of the devil. No matter what the
hardness of the territory or the indifference of
the people, if you will be true to God and stick to
the old Gospel guns, you will rout the devil, stir
Hell, and victory will come. It pays to dig.

This is a "surface age" and part of the people
are doing nothing but surface work. That is
easy, but not lasting; that is shallow, never deep;
that is sowing on stony ground, no depth of soil;
the hot sun will cook your seed; *plow deep* is
God's way, and must be ours, if we follow Him.
God knows your needs and not a few times will
answer before you pray.

Let us be prayerful, for it is only through
prayer that we can be victorious, more than
conquerors upon every battlefield. A praying
man has foresight, hence plans for the battle, and
never gets the least discouraged when things do
not break up, when things do not break loose the
first two or three weeks, but keeps drilling, drilling. He is after a well, is not digging a cistern;
an artesian well overflows winter and summer,
wet or dry; no matter about the surface, it never
depends upon the surface water.

We must take time to plant our artillery, dig
trenches, man our heavy guns, prepare the fields
for the battle. If the general gets discouraged,

grows faint-hearted, it is contagious, it will spread throughout the army and a galling defeat is inevitable. The general must be level-headed, and have cool brains; but he must be hot-hearted, for he is to cheer, encourage, enthuse the army.

Once a young sergeant came trembling, with tears in his eyes, to Napoleon, saying, "General, we are hopelessly defeated, they are ten to one." Napoleon straightened himself in his stirrups, saying, "Put me down for twenty-five thousand. I am worth twenty-five thousand men; my skill, my ingenuity is worth twenty-five thousand men. We will be victorious." And when the smoke of battle had cleared away, Napoleon's army had won one of its greatest victories. This great warrior knew how to tune his men for their greatest strength and their best fighting. In the heat of battle he was cool-headed and deliberate, never suffered himself to become nervous or the least discouraged. He enthused his army by his courage.

Even so, Christians, we must plan for the battle and where all is not sunshine and victory, then it is ours to be victorious and to encourage our weaker brethren. Prayer enables one to be of the best service to his fellows and his God. A prayerless man is a powerless man, he has no connection with the power-house, hence he is easily disheartened and put out of commission. We must be in the spirit of prayer. God hep us to *pray clear through.*

CHAPTER XXVI.

HALLIE HEALED IN ANSWER TO PRAYER.

The month of March was an ideal month. It was one of the finest we have ever seen. It was like May. The sun was warm; flowers had begun blooming; birds were singing. Mother Earth had begun to put on a carpet of green. Nature was all smiles. We were in that beautiful little town, Bertrand, Mo. God had just given us one among the best revivals of our ministry; scores had been saved; the Holy Ghost had fallen upon the saints; altars had been crowded; God had heard the midnight cries and groans of His children. The circuit had only paid $425.00, Bertrand being one of the churches, but at the close of this revival, Bertrand being a station, it paid $950.00 and had a good parsonage.

Toward the close of this revival the good people begged us to wire wife and babies to come to us. We did so, and they were with us the last week of the meeting at Bertrand, and wife sang some of her choice solos to the delight and inspiration of the great congregation.

We went from there to Parmar, Mo., and opened up a gracious meeting. The altar was full, the house was packed, and men and women were getting under tremendous conviction; confessions were being made, and the saints were getting down to earnest, wrestling prayer. On Monday morning wife woke me up at 1:30, saying, "Papa, little Hallie is very sick indeed." We called doctor, and he said, "She has an aggravated case of pneumonia." We called in two specialists and a trained nurse from Memphis, Tenn. She grew worse until one night the doctor said to us, "Brother Harney, it looks like your baby will have to die. She is growing worse, and getting weaker." They said, "We have done everything we can do. We have exhausted medical science, but this disease is so stubborn, it will not yield to medical treatment."

We threw ourselves at His feet in much fasting and heart agony; seemingly we never before got such a hold upon Him in prayer. For hours we lingered in His presence, pleading His promises, and crying, "Heal baby Hallie." Finally the doctors came to us and said, "Brother Harney, you might as well get ready and be submissive; your baby's going to die."

They had the pastor come and talk to us; they had wife come and talk to us; but we clung to God; we would not let go; we would not let up; we prayed clear through. We never had such heart agony, such soul travail, such a crushing burden as for about four days and nights, seemingly our poor heart would break. But the child grew worse. It was whispered on all sides, "The baby can't last but a few more hours." We stayed upon our knees; we clung to the promises; we cried, "Why have you thus burdened us? Why have you thus led us to agonize and wrestle for baby's healing?"

It was about four o'clock on Sunday morning. With an open Bible we were upon our face crying in heart agony, when the Holy Ghost whispered deep in our soul, "The baby is healed." We raised up and touched our wife who was in bed, and said, "Mamma, God has just given us the witness that baby Hallie is healed." Just then the nurse knocked on our door; wife said, "Come in." She opened the door, saying, "Rejoice. The fever's broken, and Hallie is much better." We said to her, "We knew that before you came, God had whispered that blessed news into our soul." The

floodtides of Heaven swept into our soul, a regular Niagara overflowed our heart, and the joy-
bells were ringing.   Oh, what peace, what joy,
filled our soul!   We shouted, we cried, we laughed, and said,

"It's just like Jesus to roll the clouds away,
   It's just like Jesus to keep us day by day."

On Thursday we brought Hallie home, and
to-day she's one of the brightest and sweetest
baby girls to us in the whole world.   She's God's;
we put her on the altar then, and we never expect
to take her off.

Reader, remember, always remember, and
never forget this one thing, that God will always
answer prayer.   He is a prayer-hearing and a
prayer-answering God.   When He places a burden upon your heart, be assured of the fact that
He will answer.   When He leads you out in
prayer, and gives you inwrought prayer, be assured of the fact that He will answer.   Let us
have heart agony; let us wrestle; let us have soul
travail; let us place our face between our knees;
let us pray clear through.   Knee work will clear
the clouds away.   Knee work will bring sunshine
into the soul.   Knee work will bring joy into our
heart and strength into our soul.   It will increase

our faith, brighten our hope, and perfect us in His
great love. Midnight wrestling will pull the fire
out of Heaven, crowd the altar, put a blistering,
burning conviction upon the sinner.

Prayer is not an easy something; it is easy to
sing, preach, or testify, but one of the hardest
things a Christian has ever done, is to pray clear
through. If you want perfect joy, if you are after
soul rest, if you want an artesian well in your
heart, *pray clear through*. If you want to live on
the mountain-top all the time, *pray clear through*.
If you want to be on the victory side constantly,
if you want to be more than conquerors, if you
want all doubts destroyed, if you would have a
richer experience, *pray clear through*. If you
want to be a soul-winner, if you want God to
honor His Word through you as an instrument,
pray clear through. If you want to be a success
in life, an honor to God and the community in
which you live, to bring your own folks to Jesus
Christ, *pray clear through*.

It will be a blessing to you to fast, to wait
upon God, to commit your way to God, to rest in
the Lord, and be filled with patience. God always
listens to the heart-broken prayer. The crying
need of this age is more who will really have soul
agony, and soul travail in prayer. We are re-

joicing to-night because of the glorious fact that
the Holy Ghost has led us into this blessed, enjoyable prayer life. Prayer feeds the soul; prayer
strengthens faith; prayer gives us power with
God and man.

CHAPTER XXVII.

A Man Knocked Blind.

It was a bitterly cold winter afternoon, deep snow covered the ground. The thermometer was hovering around 28 degrees below zero, the church was packed, a great revival was sweeping the town.

The people were so stirred and moved, so wrought upon by the Holy Spirit, that about three hundred came to one service held at three o'clock in the morning. Imagine folks leaving their warm beds and warm homes and trudging through a wintry night to that service, and some walking in about two miles from the country.

There were from forty to fifty seekers at the altar nightly. Scores were being saved and many sanctified wholly. The afternoon service we spoke of in the first paragraph was a most wonderful service. The manifestation of God's Spirit was great. Some of the Christians were so flooded with glory that they became quite noisy and a Mr. John Matthews sitting far back in the church began scoffing. We said to him, "Please do not do that," but he made a face at us. There was a large crowd of young folks near him, and we realized he was influencing them and they might consent to scoff with him, so we called the whole congregation to prayer. We prayed: "Our Father who art in heaven, this is Thy work, Thou art giving it Thy sanction, Thy Spirit is upon this meeting in marvelous power, now, we pray Thee, show this young man his sin by destroying the optic nerve for a few hours."

This prayer was breathed in us by the Holy Spirit, and we felt we must utter aloud that which was breathed into our innermost being. Right after praying this prayer, we felt that God would have us dismiss the congregation, and John with the others went his way, and we went to our room. We had not been there long, however, until Dr. Daugherty, the oculist, came running to our room, crying: "Oh, Brother Harney, John is blind, he is screaming out there in the street, the doctor is working with him. They are going to mob you." Instantly the Holy Spirit gave us the assurance and confidence that He was at work. He was answering prayer and we could rely on Him, He would see us through, so we calmly and quietly answered, "Tell the mob to come, but be sure you tell them that the first one who puts his hand on the yard gate will not only be struck blind, but paralyzed from head to foot as well." Did that mob come after such a statement as that? Never, they were afraid. They knew the Almighty God was working with John and they knew that He would protect His son.

The doctors worked eight or nine hours before John could see anything. God heard and answered the prayer of His children. As a result of this, great power fell upon the service and upon the people. They came from every direction, some of the Christians prayed all night, some fasting two or three days at a time. There was a tremendous spirit of soul agony upon the saints. One could hear the voice of prayer in almost every home, and no man dared to mock or scoff at the work of the Holy Ghost. The God of the Hebrew children, of Daniel, of the saints of all ages, was with His people. He was answering by fire.

Oh! do pause to obey the Holy Spirit, to live in such close touch with Him that He can whisper His thought into your soul and then you will dare to step out and proclaim His messages. Will you not do this? May God have the glory!

CHAPTER XXVIII.

A Circus Broken Up.

It was a beautiful sunshiny morning in October. Brother Yates and I were holding a meeting in Louisville, Ark., and this morning we decided to take a walk through the city. As we were wandering about we came to a well-beaten country road, and as we passed over the railroad tracks, we noticed they were unloading a circus. We said to Brother Yates, "This will never do. God is displeased, this circus will draw the crowd or part of it that we ought to have in the tabernacle meeting to-day; the young people, the boys and girls especially, will be so anxious to see those elephants, lions, panthers and the other wild animals, that they will go there instead of to the meeting." My soul was troubled, my spirit was pressed when strangely the Holy Spirit whispered in my heart, "Is not the same God who rolled back the Red Sea and gave Israel a dry path, who

rolled back the waters of the Jordan and gave
Israel dry footing, is not this same God, who
quenched the fiery furnace, who locked the lions'
mouths, answered Elijah's cry in Mt. Carmel, is
not He able to stop this circus?" Yes! So tenderly the Holy Spirit whispered, "Cannot you
pray clear through; cannot you get a grip upon
God? Cannot you place your face between your
knees? Will not God answer your heart's cry?
Is He not the same yesterday, to-day and forever?" "Before he calls I will answer." Dare to
trust Him. "Ask, and ye shall receive," and if
two agree it shall be done.

  We turned our steps homeward, or rather to
our room, and went before God in earnest, protracted soul agony. There was a crushing burden on our hearts. We felt that God would be
true to His promise if we could get hold of that
promise and make it ours. Somehow the Spirit
pressed us more and more urging us on, urging
us to pray and helping us to take hold on God.
Finally, from the depths of our spirits, we began
crying, "Lord, send a cyclone! Lord, send a cyclone! Tear up that circus tent, teach these god-
less church-members a lesson, open their eyes and
help them to see their sin, help them to see what
it means to leave a meeting with altars crowded

with broken-hearted seekers and go to a circus."
The more we prayed, the more we wanted to pray;
we could not let go the horns of the altar, it
seemed we had to pray until we prayed clear
through; we had to pray until we heard from the
God of Heaven; we had to pray until the answer
came. After a time, Brother Yates said, "I must
go to the tabernacle and practise some new
songs," but the Holy Spirit kept us on our faces
and we continued to pray. Just before noon, God
gave us a wonderful, glorious vision.

There on our knees, by faith, we could see the
black stormclouds gathering, we could hear the
thunder rolling, we could see the lightning flashing. The Holy Spirit said in unmistakable terms,
"God has answered your cry and the cyclone is
coming. The circus tent will be broken down.
The people will be taught a lesson, God will be
honored, sinners convicted and blinded church-
members will have scales drop from their eyes."
After God gave us this promise, we arose from
our knees, our spirit was satisfied, we knew that
God was working.

We went to dinner at the boarding-house and
after partaking of the meal arose and announced
the fact that, in answer to prayer, God would
send a cyclone that afternoon about two o'clock.

Some of the folks took it seriously, others laughed and mocked at the idea. Still others said God would not answer such a prayer, and others advised, "You had best wait and see, for it is only two hours now if the cyclone comes at two o'clock; you will not have so long to wait." We went back to our rooms, once again to our knees, and began crying to God not to fail us. We had given forth His message, we had publicly stated that which the Holy Spirit had whispered in our hearts, and now we plead with Him to see us through. Again the Spirit whispered and assured us, "It is coming. Wait." "They that wait upon the Lord shall renew their strength."

We went to the afternoon service, sang one hymn, prayed one prayer, gave a few minutes talk, and then there was a terrific clap of thunder announcing the fact that the cyclone was coming. We said to the people, "Hurry to your homes, the storm is on." What forked lightning! what black clouds! Men and women rushed homeward, some screamed aloud, and all in a terrible fright. It was an awful hour, the circus had just been opened. The cyclone struck the circus tent and tore it wide open and down went the center pole. The people were rushing homeward in the wildest confusion. That night we had hundreds at the tabernacle, God had awakened the people to realize that He still answers prayer. Those who laughed and scoffed at our announcement of God sending a cyclone were put to shame. God got the glory.

Oh, dare to trust Him, He will answer prayer. He has never failed us, but in order to have the answer, we must wait, we must have patience, we must pray clear through. Jesus will answer prayer. Will we call upon Him? Will we hold fast until He gives the witness that the answer is coming? We can have it if we will.

CHAPTER XXIX.

A MERRY-GO-ROUND PUT OUT OF COMMISSION IN ANSWER TO PRAYER.

On a warm night in early fall, we began a revival in Compton, Ky. This is an inland town and the people simply went wild when any attractions came to town. The church was cold, frozen up; all the members but three had gone out of the religious business; nothing doing. The young folks did about as they pleased, there was quite a bit of drinking and lots of profanity, and novel reading was the craze. The town has only about five hundred souls and some of them did not act one bit like they had a soul.

Our first sight of this old town made our heart ache. Oh! what a burden came upon us; we saw at once that we had a tough proposition ahead. The first night five souls met us at the church. It was a big church and it looked so lonely; just five, no more. Just as we began read-

ing our text, a merry-go-round, on a vacant lot
just by the church, began a fearful whistling, and
kept it up; we could not hear ourselves read, and
we know no one else could. About this time, right
on the opposite side of the church, a medical-show
brass band began and we were between brass
band and merry-go-round. We saw it was useless for us to try to preach. Some would slip up,
look in and laugh. My what a crowd! It looked
for a moment like we were defeated, as though
we might as well quit, they could drown us all out.

We closed our Bible and said, "Let us pray."
While in prayer, the Spirit whispered, "Why not
pray clear through and get God to blow that merry-go-round out of business?" We laughed, we
praised God, and after prayer, we said, "Now,
the Lord can put that merry-go-round out of business and run this medical fake out of town. Who
will join us in a fast and in praying clear through
for the mighty God to undertake for us, in this
awful battle?" Some one on the outside laughed,
others said, "Oh! such praying can not be answered," but four of us went to earnest prayer.
We prayed for three days and the fire fell. One
sister came running in, where we were stopping,
shouting, "I have the witness. God will blow that
merry-go-round up."

That night, as it had leaked out about the saints wrestling in prayer, there was a tremendous crowd at the merry-go-round, and my! it did set up a fearful whistle, defying God. It seemed more determined than ever to show us how much noise it could make. That night our crowd was 120, one could feel God as soon as you entered the church door; the place was awful. How the singing did thrill us! We were about ready to read our text, when there was a frightful explosion—screams, and how the crowd did pour into that church! The merry-go-round had blown up! In a few moments the news reached the medical-show tent, fright took hold of that gang and quiet filled that place. Men whispered, "I tell you God is answering prayer and all had best keep out of the way." That night the altar was full, one sister lay under the power for hours. Next night the church was packed, until scores were turned away, one hundred were at the altar and many were saved. This meeting ran three weeks, and people drove ten miles at night to get to that devil-driving, soul-saving revival.

The saints simply took God at His word; they prayed through, and felt He was able to clear all obstacles out of His way. When you go to pray, go believing, not doubting, for He is able. He can, if you will pray, and not faint, but wait. We waited three days, but it paid. Many times God is defeated because there is no one who will dare to *pray through*. There are hindrances to praying clear through, such as getting our eyes on the surroundings. That is why Peter went down, he got his eyes off of Jesus, upon the waves, then fear gripped him, doubts filled his mind, and down he went. Our eyes must be stayed, fixed, riveted on Him. Joshua did not look at the towering walls, but at Jesus. Moses did not look at the Red Sea, but to Him, and He opened up the way for Israel to go over dryshod. So we dared not look at our environments; we had to trust, not watch; we did not look, but we cried to Jesus.

Often you look at things which are not real. In traveling over Western Texas, you will see ahead, always ahead, lakes, but there are none to be found, they are not real, so the devil will pile up mountains until, if you will let them, they will overwhelm you, deplete your strength and rob you of a great victory. If they are real, He can make you an overcomer. The fiery furnace was real, but God went in with the three Hebrew children. The Red Sea was real, but He opened a dry path. The walls around Jericho were real, but He tore them down, and, too, without any dynamite or powder. We could not have gained for Him this blessed victory had we looked or listened; we cried, we believed, and the merry-go-round was put out of commission and the medical show took fright and fled.

We must keep our eyes on Jesus and ever remember that He is fully able to undo all the things that old Splitfoot has ever done. Amen! Glory! Again, we are not to give our ears over to the devil, he will whisper, "towering walls, mountain-top waves, you are not able, not qualified, have too many weaknesses, a stammering speech, you are slow, you cannot do this and you will fail at the other." He is good at making suggestions, he is full of such, but listen! God's call sounds out loudly, *if you are willing.* He is able, the cattle upon a thousand hills are His, He has the ready, needed cash; if you need strength, He has tons of it, miles of it; if you lack power, He is full. Get Him and you get power, power to live a clean, happy life, and power for service, until you will be as free as a lark.

Defeat comes only to those who will listen to the devil. Achan listened, then took the gold, the garment, and was killed. Cain listened, and became the first murderer. Judas gave the devil his ear, then sold his Christ, hung himself and is burning in Hell to-day.

One can not be defeated who lives upon his knees; knee work brings victory day by day, until your life is filled with fruitfulness; you are here. yonder, visiting the sick, praying with the broken-hearted, scattering good books, papers or tracts. The prayer life is a victorious life, because your ears are deaf to Satan's whispers; you are off of the shady side of the damp street; you are enabled to bring things to pass for God and poor weak, lost humanity. One can live—yes, really *live*—in a constant spirit of earnest prayer, and this knocks the bottom out of Heaven and fills you with perfect delight. Your experience will be satisfactory, your faith strong, and then it will be easy to work in His vineyard.

There are many weaklings in God's harvest-field, all because they hurry, rush into battle without any discipline or preparation, they have never tarried, waited, hence many leave the ministry, and go to other professions, all because they failed in knee work.

Knee work always prepares one to be useful in God's cause. There will be no drones, not one. A praying man is no drone, never! he's a live bee, making lots of good honey, his beehive full all the

time, winter or summer, not only in a revival,
not only when the preacher is around, but all the
time; there are no dark, gloomy, blue days, neither any weather-breeders; but *all* days will be brim-
full of sunshine.   We make our life successful or
a failure.   A preacher once said to the author,
"Oh! some were cut out to be successful, some to
be failures."   I said, "Never! a man has to do
with himself."   The apostles, before the ten-days
prayer-meeting, only cast out a few devils, raised
a few dead folk, healed a few sick folk, but within fifty minutes after that ten-days prayer-meeting, they won three thousand souls.   Success
comes by prayer, by waiting, not by looking at
environments, not by watching others, but by
earnest, prevailing prayer.   God can give any one
success who will take the time to wrestle, fast,
cry to Him until the fire falls.   He is able, He is
willing, then why not pray, and pray *now?*   Why
go on meeting defeats, why not defeat the devil
by *praying clear through?*

CHAPTER XXX.

SEVEN MISSIONARIES AND THEIR FAMILIES HOUSED, FED, AND CLOTHED THROUGH PRAYER.

This is one of the leading camps of the great Southwest. The tabernacle has a seating capacity of thirty-seven hundred; the choir loft five hundred. Here we hear the best singers of the world. We have seen the thousands moved not only to tears by the great singers, but to holy enthusiasm and to much rejoicing. We have seen 25,000 people in front of and around the preacher; they come from all parts. Several hundred camp in shacks and tents and at all hours one hears the voice of prayer, praise, and rejoicing. The people are of the common classes, but honest and full of industry; they believe in God, in Jesus Christ and the operations of the Holy Ghost. They teach that Jesus Christ is stronger than the devil, in that He can undo anything old

Splitfoot has ever done, that is, save His people from all sin.

They not only preach this, but in their humble homes, they honor Christ by a devout, commendable life—commendable, may be, not in the eyes of man, but in the eyes of God. Man sees in us that for which he is looking; God looks at the motives. One may be full of mistakes and blunders, but have a good heart.

In a certain year the author was the leading preacher at this camp; he had a good opportunity to see these good people at close range, to study their methods and work, and all proved conclusively that they had been with Jesus. One Sunday morning, in the presence of twenty to thirty thousand people, the author had preached about ten minutes when that mighty preacher, Dr. A. A. Niles, went down into the aisle and picked up a rubber-tired invalid chair, with what, to us, looked like an invalid in it. He carried chair and invalid on to the platform, saying, "Mr. Harney, listen." We turned and looked into a very bright-faced woman. Her face was lit up with Heaven's light. She had an angelic expression. We felt that we were right in the presence of one of those quiet, unassuming holy women who had constant connection with the

skies, who was always hitched up to the power-
house, who could get through to God any minute.
As we turned toward her, she threw up her hand
shouting, "I have the Blessing." It was wonderful, it was melting. Stout men and women wept
all over that great audience. She simply was
living in the center of His will. It was not so
much what she said as how she said it. She was
simply swallowed up in the will of God. She had
but one job and that was to please her Heavenly
Father.

After preaching and exhorting, several scores
rushed to the altar. She said to her chair woman,
"Wheel me to the seekers," then she reached
over and took one man by the shoulder, telling
him to turn to her mourner's bench (the wheel of
her chair), and soon he was shouting. She went
to seven and all of them got through brightly.

After the service, I asked her for the privilege of going with her to dinner. I asked, "Are
you never discouraged? Don't you look at other
women with good limbs, a strong body, and wonder why you were so badly deformed? Do you
ever bring any accusations against Him?"

She said, "Brother Harney, never, not once.
I am rejoicing that I am just as I am. Had I
been otherwise, I might have been like thousands

of other women—in sin, but praise the Lord! as
it is, I am full of faith, hope, and salvation. I
am doing a great work for God and lost humanity. I spend from two to three hours almost
every day reading my Bible and in prayer. I am
having the time of my life in serving the Lord,
He is so good, so patient, so forbearing, so longsuffering with me. I am so unworthy of His
great love and mercy. He simply fills my heart
continuously with His perfect love. Had I been
a strong woman, I could have been useless and
fruitless. Have you ever thought how many able-
bodied, bright-minded people are on the broad
road to destruction? So I am praising God to-
day, yes, I am really delighted, that I am just as
I am, for my life is like a Florida flower garden,
like a California orange grove. I am just as
happy, just as contented as it is possible for mor-
tal to be. I am perfectly satisfied, because I know
that I am as God wanted me to be, and I am ful-
filling His purpose relative to my life's work much
better as I am than I could have done had I been
a strong, able-bodied woman. I am living on the
sunny side of the street.

"The Bible is the most interesting book I can
study. Its pages loom up with beautiful promises
before me as I read, until my soul is immersed

and swallowed up in the warm gulf stream of His
fullness.   It becomes more precious day by day.
I get so hungry to get alone before Him with the
open Bible.   How it feeds, how it strengthens,
how it comforts.   When the devil whispers, "Defeat awaits you," I just open the Bible and read
how God conquered through Daniel, how God
defeated the enemy through Gideon's three hundred, how God tore down the towering walls of
Jericho by the blast of the rams' horns, then I feel
like I could leap through a troop and with the
jawbone of an ass slay a thousand.   You know
it isn't always with the strong that He conquers.
Look at His disciples; they were unlettered men.
Again, through the crowing of one rooster, God
brought back into the fold the spokesman of the
apostolic college of bishops.   God takes the weak
things to confound the mighty.

"You see in working through these simple
channels, He gets all the glory, and He is jealous
of having the glory and will use all who will give
Him the glory.   How could I be discouraged
when my Lord is using me to do such a tremendous work?   To-day I have in foreign lands, working among the heathen, bringing hundreds of
them to Christ, seven missionaries, and we are
seeing annually hundreds of these poor, sin-

cursed, devil-driven heathen lifted into the beautiful light of forgiveness. Oh, it is wonderful just
to read my mail! How these missionaries thrill
my very soul by telling me what great things our
Christ is doing. Just a few weeks ago one of my
men closed a month's campaign in which five or
six thousand knelt for prayer and professed faith
in God. Remember, it isn't hard to get a thous-
and people out at a six o'clock morning service."

We broke in by asking if her parents were
millionaires; we wanted to know how she could
carry on this great missionary work unless her
parents were wealthy; how she could do so much
and be thus deformed? She said, "My parents
are dead and I have no wealthy kinsman who
helps me, but I take my Bible and go before Him
telling Him just how much money my men need,
not how much they want, not how much they are
urging me to send them, but, how much does He
see they need to carry on His work. He has
never failed to answer. When we pray we must
get His mind and pray for the thing that will
glorify Him most and bring the most fruits for
His glory. Too many times we go to prayer
without any forethought, without any burden,
without any definite leading, hence, we get befogged, bemuddled, and then it is that we are so

easily misguided and misled and not a few times
bring disrepute to His cause.

"I never pray until I first get quiet before Him
and wait for His Holy Spirit to burden or to lead
me out along the line He wants me to go, and
then I hold on, wait, patiently wait, not getting
in a hurry, wrestle, Jacob-like, until the break of
day, fast and pray three days and nights, Esther-
like, until I hear from God. When He sees in
us no selfishness, no selfish purpose, that all that
we plan to do is done wholly for His glory, then
it is He will answer. And we must not make
too much noise and give too much publicity, because it might bring inflation. We must be
guarded and very cautious that our praying,
preaching, testifying, singing and devotion to
Him and His work are all done with an eye
single to His glory, and never lift up before the
people any talent that we may possess. Humility
and meekness are rich graces, graces that will
flood one's soul with Heaven's golden sunlight,
causing one to ride the waves of perfect love continuously.

"My work is done through much prayer. He
has always kept enough money in the treasury
just to keep us going, and sometimes we have to
wrestle a week before the clouds rift, but oh.

what blessed victory comes into one's life with
such waiting! what strength! how stalwart the
faith! how towering the hope! how rich the experience that floods one's soul and carries him
out into mid ocean, into the bottomless experience
of a full salvation! It would never be for our
good for God to answer us at all times quickly.
We would grow lazy, become idle and lose out in
the prayer life. God knows, for our good and
His glory, that He must at times withhold the
answer for a while. We never grow as much
in grace as in one of these prayer battles. It is
here that we make religious muscles, it is here
we toughen fiber, it is here we become strong,
stalwart warriors.

"Show me men of much prayer and we will
always see men who move things for God and
lost humanity. Look at A. B. Simpson, who
prayed all night at Old Orchard, Me., and took
a collection of over $100,000 next morning as
a missionary offering. He got that by wrestling
all night in heart agony. A few years ago this
man of God had more missionaries in the field
than all the rest of Christendom. God honors,
blesses, and uses men who live on their faces."

That Sunday afternoon, as that blessed man
of God, Ed. Fergerson, was reading his text, this

little woman threw up her hands and raised a shout, the dark clouds had rifted, she had prayed through and victory like a Niagara was sweeping her soul. One man jumped out of the choir, ran down the aisle and threw a twenty-dollar bill in her lap. Here came five others down one aisle, here came six sisters, and then a commotion, the power swept the audience, two to three hundred stood waving their handkerchiefs and rejoicing for the ten or fifteen minutes during which this hallelujah storm lasted.

This little woman kept looking up into His face saying, "Much obliged, Lord." Some two to three hundred dollars were pitched into her lap. She had been with Jesus, He knew her needs, we did not, and He answered in a most remarkable manner. The Lord knew that a little church was needed and that one of her men could do ten times the good if he had a church home, so here came this shower of money, but not until this saint had wrestled and cried—*prayed clear through.*

CHAPTER XXXI.

Praying without Ceasing.

I Thessalonians 5:17.

The Apostle Paul, that learned disciple of Jesus Christ, tells us in this Scripture how to keep pace with God. Light is given for us to walk in, and when we fail to do so, darkness crowds our hearts. The light given here on the all-important subject of prayer, is very beneficial.

A train must have power to pull it down the track. Steam is the power, but this power comes from water and fire. A Christian's vital force comes through the prevailing spirit of prayer; not a spell of praying to-day, and then a gap of ten days, but a continuance in prayer. We must be in the Spirit and have the spirit of prayer moment by moment. God never lavishes His power upon an unfaithful or an unwise servant.

This does not mean that we are to be upon our

knees all the time; neither does it mean audible
praying all the time; but a spirit of prayer, a spirit
of devotion. A man may not be making mani-
festations of his love for his wife all the time, but
he loves her nevertheless.

A man may be immersed in business, his
shoulders bearing up great burdens; or a woman
may have her hands full in the nursery or elsewhere, but still a constant spirit of prayer may
be going up from their hearts, like incense from
the altar. Niagara flows day and night, winter
and summer; so is the spirit of prayer from the
heart of every true Christian.

Many rich blessings crowd into the heart during the busy hours of the day, because of this
blessed spirit of prayer. Faces have lit up, eyes
have brimmed full, lips been quivering, because
of this blessed, constant, holy communion, and
that, too, while the man or woman was engaged
in daily toil.

This constant prayerfulness is why some people old in years never grow old in reality, and
never lose their usefulness. A praying man always bears fruit, and the more he prays, the
more earnestly he prays, the more fruit he will
bear. Neglect of prayer means a loss of usefulness. Failure to pray grieves the Spirit, and a

Christian can do nothing for God and lost humanity without the Spirit, for it is He who makes groanings through us that can not be made by lips of clay.

A sainted old woman, who had read and reread the Bible through more than a score of times, was laughing one day, with the open Bible lying on her lap, when a neighbor walked in. The neighbor said, "Grandmother, why are you so happy?" "Oh," said Grandmother, "I was just having my usual chat with my Father. I find such a joy, such a deep, abiding, constant, sweet peace in reading the Word, and in prayer, that I never get lonesome, and haven't been discouraged since the Holy Ghost came into my life in His fullness. My son and his wife go to the office early each morning, but I always have company, the best of company. I have good times all the time; haven't had a 'blue Monday' in twenty-five years. My God has never failed me. He has been so patient, so forbearing, so longsuffering with me, a poor frail woman. His thoughts toward me are good. He smiles upon me all the time. My room is filled with His sunshine, and my heart is crowded full of His perfect love. I am simply having a heaven on earth to go to Heaven in. I committed my way to God twenty-five years ago and I have not worried one moment since, not once. He is able to take care of me; He has promised to do it; and He is faithful.

"I only have this rich experience, this strong faith, this bright hope, because of the constant spirit of prayer, for I pray all the time, that is, I am in the spirit of prayer."

A person's love for God increases as the spirit of prayer grows.

Nehemiah went forth in great strength, and succeeded in what seemed to many an impossibility—in rebuilding the walls of Jerusalem. The workmen did faithful work, and everything went smoothly on, even though the devil tried hard to discourage, and to block Nehemiah's pathway. Why? Because Nehemiah was a man who had prayed and fasted much, and had the mind of God before he went forth.

The reason why so many of us fail is because we hurry into battle without the slightest preparation, and so lead our gifts and talents and usefulness to the slaughter-pen. Had the disciples rushed into the world's harvest-field from Bethany, they would have made an awful failure. They needed and must have a ten-days prayer-meeting. Waiting develops one's patience, gives time for reflection, and an opportunity for confession and repentance; so these men must tarry.

Theirs was plenty of work to do; men were dying, jails were crowded, but Jesus said, *"Wait."* He knew that that ten-days prayer-meeting would put into their lives such a force, such a power, such liberty and freedom, that they would go forth destroying the works of the devil, and having constant, real victory all the time.

This waiting brought the purging into their lives, hence they were qualified to bring forth thirty, sixty, and a hundred fold. That is why Peter, on the Day of Pentecost, preached a sermon that put three thousand souls on God's side. He could never have done this before that ten-days prayer-meeting; it could only follow the prayer-meeting.

Christ and His three disciples were on the Mount of Transfiguration, then, *after that,* He came down and cast a devil out of a boy. Christ prayed upon another mountain until the grey streaks of dawn could be seen in the east, then He came down, quieted a mad sea, a raging storm, saved his disciples from the horrors of a mad typhoon, and rescued Peter from a watery grave.

Peter prayed and saw a great vision, then went down to the house of Cornelius and preached with such freedom, such boldness, such sweetness of spirit, that a great revival broke out, and the entire household of Brother Cornelius was saved.

Paul and Silas held a midnight prayer-meeting in the Philippian jail; then the power of God fell so mightily, that there was such a concussion, such an earthquake, that the old jailer awoke and grabbed his sword, saying, "They have all fled, and I'll be accused of letting them escape, so I'll kill myself." But Paul shouted, "Do thyself no harm, for there isn't a 'Come-outer' among us; we are all here." The jailer and his household were all converted, so that prayer-meeting of Paul and Silas stirred things and woke them up.

God honors prayer that comes from the heart; let it be in a hovel, hut, jail or temple, He will answer true prayer.

Paul knew full well how to discuss, how to preach, how to write about praying, for he himself was a man of much prayer. Once, when seemingly all were going to destruction, to a watery grave, he prayed and the Spirit whispered, "Not one shall be lost." So he stood up and told them that, although they had gone contrary to light given, although they had misjudged him, yet not one of them should be lost. Paul got this message through earnest prayer.

Many to-day walk in golden sunlight, bathe

their souls in crystal waters, live in God's flower gardens, walk hand in hand, as Enoch of old, with God, because they live in the spirit of prayer. We can split the clouds, thaw the ice, melt the snow, defeat the devil, span the chasm, climb the mountain, if we are in the spirit of prayer. We can crowd altars with weeping penitents, bring multitudes to God, break up dens of vice, destroy "King Alcohol," if we have the spirit of prayer.

God uses all who have this vital, this real, this earnest, this constant spirit of prayer. Let us quit trifling, and *pray clear through.*

CHAPTER XXXII.

SOUL REST.

"Thou wilt keep him in perfect peace, whose mind is stayed on thee: because he trusteth in thee." (Isaiah 26:3.)

The great prophet Isaiah discloses the fact in this verse that, if we are kept in perfect peace, it is because we trust in God. It is the trusting that brings the peace. Faith in God anchors our mind to Him. Faith is to salvation what the mainspring is to a watch. Here is a beautiful watch, with seventeen jewels made by a master smith, but it would be worthless without the mainspring, for, mark you, the mainspring is the life, the dynamo, the power that throws the hands around the dial plate, and points out the correct time of day. If the mainspring were to snap, the watch would stop suddenly. The case has nothing to do with the mechanism or the running of this time-keeper. You may place the works of the watch in a wooden case, or a sawdust case, or a tin case, and it will tick the correct time of day. The case is only the house in which the watch lives.

We said faith is to salvation what the mainspring is to the watch. Faith is that power, that factor in one's life, that moves him out for God. It matters not what kind of a house he is clothed with or lives in. We mean by this, the woman or man with strong faith in God may have a delicate, diseased body, but still be a power. We knew a woman who had great faith in God; through her prayers revivals were started in the community, and the fire prayed out of Heaven, yet the doctors told us that she had a tumor in her stomach that weighed twenty to thirty pounds, and she was one of the incurables. But her face was aways shining and she was always rejoicing.

We saw a little woman who was wheeled in under the shed at Bonnie Campground, and if we were rightly informed, she only weighed about eighty pounds. She had no lower limbs, and no use of one of her hands. Yet this little woman was praising God all the time. Her face fairly shone. We saw her in her wheel chair at the altar instructing the penitents. She was instru-

mental in one service in pointing seven strong
men to the cross. She had four or five missionaries in the foreign field. We said to her, "How
do you keep your men in the mission fields?" She
said, "By faith in God." She was one of the
worst deformed people we ever saw, yet she had
faith that was strong, and laughed impossibilities
in the face, and did mighty things for God.

Faith is to salvation what steam is to the
engine. We have often walked around the old
Jumbo engine, handled the cow-catcher, when
there was no water, no fire and no steam, but be
it understood, when the boiler is full of water, and
the steam chest is pulsating with steam, and the
pop valve is blowing off, and that old train is rac-
ing down the track ninety miles per hour, crying
out, "Clear the road, I'm coming!" we always
clear the road, for it has run over many a fellow
because he did not get out of the way. As we
were going out of a city in Texas one morning,
we heard the screaming of the engine. We raised
our window just in time to see an old jennet and
her colt going through the air, and the train trot-
ting on down the track thirty or forty miles per
hour, as if it had only struck a gnat.

A man or woman full of the Holy Ghost and
faith can chase the devil and make him clear the

track, for one such can put a thousand to flight, and two can chase ten thousand. Samson, with strong faith, and the jawbone of an ass, slew his thousands. David, with a Gibraltar faith in God, a sling and five pebbles, brought the great Goliath to the ground. Gideon, whose faith did not stagger, with three hundred brave warriors put to flight the fields full of enemies. Shadrach, Meshach and Abed-nego, who had living faith in God, never doubted once but what God would take care of them in the fiery furnace, and bring them out more than conquerors.

"Faith is the substance of things hoped for; an evidence of things not seen." Faith is that power in man that reaches away out into the unseen and pulls things up and looks at them. Faith is that power in man that goes away out into the unfelt regions and brings the things up and handles them. Faith makes stairways up every mountain, bridges every chasm, spikes Hell's artillery, and brings things to pass for God.

We must step out upon God's promises, for "He that believeth on the Son of God hath the witness in himself." We do not pray clear through by *feeling,* but by *faith.* We do not live by *sight,* but by *faith,* and God will be careful to see to it that those who step out upon His promises and trust Him will never sink beneath the mad waves. Faith illuminates the long, dark tunnels. Faith lightens the burden, brightens hope, and draws Heaven close; faith in God, not in environments, not in the arm of flesh, but a living faith, a faith that brings results, a faith that has fruits.

Why should we doubt just because we cannot see or feel? Why should we doubt when things do not go just as we planned? Why not stand still and see the salvation of God? When He commands, we should obey whether or not we see or feel. The greatest blessing comes to those who trust Him, who step out upon His promises in spite of environments, who, in spite of feelings, look up into His face and say, "I *can*, I *will*, I *do* believe." Keep repeating it, "I *do* believe," "I *will* believe." Keep saying it, "I am *determined* to trust. I will *not* doubt." Doubts damn; doubts destroy; doubts blind; doubts brings gloom and defeat. We *will* believe. We *must* believe. We *do* believe. Count on His word. We trust Thee now.

How sweet it will be when the desired haven is reached, when we can look up into His dear face and say, "Lord, thou dost know that we trusted Thee every step of the way." We should

not want the Lord to give us candies or wrap a
little sugar up in a rag, but we, as His children,
should take Him at His word.   His word is
enough. Then, why not look up and say to-day,
"My faith looks up to Thee, Thou dear Lamb
of Calvary"? A child that a parent has to hire is
not an obedient child; that is, the child has not the
proper regard, the proper love for the parent.   If
you should say, "Mary, please bring me a drink
of water," and she should say, "I will, papa, for
ten cents," it would grieve your heart, and pain
your soul. So when you see an open door, or feel
led out, or want some blessing, and you cry to
God to first give you the feelings or the witness,
it grieves God, it injures your own experience.
The Lord save us from wanting the assurance—
the candies, the nuts! Let us walk in the light,
obey the injunctions, and God will see to it that
we will get the blessings needed. It means much
to simply take Him at His word, simply leave all
in His hands, and step out on the promise and
reckon it is done, get up and go on and act like it
is really done, without the assurance. If you
have done your part, walked in all the light God
has given, you can step out on His promise and
He will never fail you. The things you really
need will be yours to enjoy.

Sometimes when you really believe, the thing looks darker and gets much darker, but that should never shake your faith, that should never cause you to tremble once. Just stand still and Red Seas will open up, the Jordan will give you a dry road, the walls of Jericho will fall, the fiery furnaces will be quenched, and lions' mouths will be locked, for God honors faith, and "we are saved by faith, through grace, and that not of ourselves, it is the gift of God."

It pleases God for us to trust Him, trust Him without teasing for assurances, without teasing for the witness; trust Him where we cannot see; trust Him when there are not any feelings. You trust your friends. You believe their word. You do not ask them for a witness. You trust your child to the doctor, to the nurse, and oftentimes they are not worthy of trust, so can you not trust your soul to God, the great God who gave His Son to die on the rugged tree for you, and who wants to flood your soul with joy and peace? But this only comes through faith. You cannot get any blessing without faith, for faith brings the blessing. "It is impossible to please God without faith." "Have faith in God." It is not works, but faith. When you have faith, then you will be a good worker.

We must believe if we expect to receive, for it is first believe, then receive. You cannot get the witness to a thing before the thing is accomplished. The witness always comes after the transaction. When you receive the witness that you are saved, you were saved before the Holy Ghost said you were. When you receive the witness that you are sanctified, you were sanctified before the Spirit said so. When you receive the blessed witness that you are healed, you were healed before the witness. Why? You are saved, sanctified and healed by faith, and after you have believed, then the Spirit comes and witnesses to the glorious fact.

"They that wait upon God renew their strength: they mount up on wings as eagles; they run and are not weary, they walk and do not faint." "He that believeth on the Son hath the witness in himself: he that believeth not God hath made him a liar, because he believeth not the record that God gave of his Son." Now, if you doubt, you make God a liar. But if you believe on the Son, you have the witness in your own heart. Do not look for signs and wonders, but simply have faith in God.

Peter went down because of his doubts. Peter denied and cursed God because of his fear.

Shadrach, Meshach, and Abed-nego were delivered from the fiery furnace because of their faith
in God. John was taken care of on the Isle of
Patmos because of an unflinching faith. Elijah
was fed out on Juniper Circuit because he was
trusting God. God will take care of those who
trust Him. It is impossible to pray through unless you have a faith that laughs impossibilities
in the face, that stands flat-footedly upon God's
immutable Word without a flinch. It is impossible to get the ear of God in earnest prayer unless
you have a faith that will not be deterred; a live
faith, a wide-awake faith. The greatest hindrance to praying clear through is a failure to
simply look up into the face of Jesus Christ, and
say, "I do trust you." It is not, "I *will*," but "I
do, now and here." It is the *present* faith that
counts. It is the present faith that brings victory.

CHAPTER XXXIII.

PREVAILING PRAYER THE KEY TO THE GREATEST VICTORIES POSSIBLE TO THE CHURCH OF GOD IN THIS WORLD.

(Selected from "Prevailing Prayer, or, The Secret of Soul-winning," by Rev. E. Wigle.)

In the way of him who would understand the subject of prayer more perfectly than the vast majority of Christians, there are difficulties that at times will embarrass him—sometimes greatly embarrass him, for this is a subject of unmeasured height, and depth, and breadth. Its relations and potency in the Divine administration no one can fully understand. Many millions of prayers are sincerely offered but never answered, and the perplexing question arises: Why? While prayer is set forth in the Word of God as a privilege, yet multitudes feel it to be a burden; get discouraged and cease to pray.

238

Encouragements to Pray.

While there are numerous mysteries to be solved and difficulties to be overcome by him who would thread the ever onward and upward pathway of prayer, far beyond where the feet of the vast majority have borne them to the sacred heights and rapturous visions of the mount of transfiguration, and so near to Heaven itself as hardly to know whether in or out of it, yet such are the encouragements and helps to pray, and such its rewards that, comparatively, the difficulties dwindle to almost nothing. There are, to the schoolboy, numerous and great difficulties in mastering problems in arithmetic, but he can master them if he will. If he does, he grows intellectually; if he does not, development ceases. We are all pupils in the school of prayer, and the Great Teacher has purposely, in infinite love and wisdom, so framed the problem in the text book of prayer, as to make it necessary to persevere against all difficulties and master the mysterious problems as they come.

Keep At It.

All that is necessary to succeed, is to *keep at it*, and *keep at it*, and *keep at it*, praying "without ceasing," "praying always," and one difficulty after another will disappear, dissolved in sweetest blessing to the heart. A young minister, who was very desirous of becoming very successful in winning souls, asked Harrison, the evangelist, how he might become such a soul-winner. Harrison replied, *"Keep at it."* So Jesus says to the praying soul: "Men ought always to pray and not faint." "Oh, what blessed heights are reached, and what ravishing visions burst upon the sight of the soul who perseveres and makes these difficulties stepping-stones to victory after victory, "looking unto Jesus, the author and finisher of his faith."

THE END OF PRAYER IS OUR GOOD.

Prayer is not offered on the presumption that God is unacquainted with our wants, or that our supplications can occasion any change in His nature. On these principles it is obvious that prayer must have been instituted for our benefit.

WHAT IS PRAYER?

The question very properly arises: What is prayer? It is not an invention. It has its birth in the first sigh, the first tear, the first felt want of man. Prayer is the soul conversing with God. It is the appointed means of communion between God and man, by which the creature tells his

wants to the great Father, who alone can satisfy
the longings of the soul.   It is as natural for
Christians to pray as for a child to go to its
earthly parent and ask for bread.   Prayer indeed
is the "crying of an infant in the night."   It is
putting up our little hands into God's all powerful hand.   It is the opening of our mouths, like
birds in the nest, to receive their food.   It is born
of our need from the heart, the womb of the soul.
Prayer is the most essential act of private devotion and public worship, in all ages and nations.
It is rooted and grounded in man's moral and
religious constitution, enjoined by God and com-
mended by the highest examples.   It is speaking
to God, and offering to Him our petitions for
mercies needed, and our thanks for mercies obtained.   It embraces invocation, supplication, intercession and thanksgiving.   It may be mental,
vocal, private or public; in the closet, in the family, or in the house of God.   We may pray for
ourselves and others, for things needful to body
or soul.   All the saints of God were fervent and
mighty in prayer.   The objections to prayer pro-
ceed from atheistic and fatalistic theories.   It is
more natural for God, who is infinitely merciful,
to answer the prayers of His children, than that
earthly parents should grant the requests of their

children. (Matt. 7: 11.) Our prayers were fore-
seen by Him like all other free acts and included
in His eternal plan. In spite of all objections
men pray on.

GOD'S WILL AND PRAYER.

Prayer depends on God's will, but does not
determine it. Man appeals, God complies. Man
asks, God grants.

SUBJECTIVE VALUE OF PRAYER.

"Prayer has a subjective value necessary to
individual piety, produces solemnity, enlightens
and quickens the conscience, teaches dependence,
gives true views of God, and produces such a
change in us as renders it consistent for Him to
change His course toward us."

THE WOUNDED SOLDIER'S PRAYERS.

"An army surgeon once illustrated prayer by
narrating his experience on a battlefield, after a
terrific conflict. 'The ground', he said, 'was covered with the dead and wounded. There was
work enough for twenty surgeons to do. It was
doleful to hear their cries. One cried out: 'Surgeon, I am bleeding to death! Won't you please
bind up this artery?' Another, 'My limb is brok-
en? Won't you take me to the hospital?' And

still another: 'Surgeon, surgeon, I am in awful pain, can't you give me some anodyne?' And so, all over the field, each individual was asking according to his own personal need. They were praying: 'Send the physician.' Yes, that is prayer when each person who feels the hurt and wounds inflicted by sin, comes to Christ, the Divine Physician, and asks Him to heal his wounds. Such prayer has faith in it. Those soldiers expected the surgeon to help them. They knew that he was there for that purpose, and they asked in faith, nothing doubting. They threw themselves, wounded and bleeding, on the mercy and skill of the surgeon. Equally practical, is all true prayer. 'Lord, help me, here is my guilt, etc., I lay it all upon Thee.' It charges Christ with all, and leaves everything to Him. It is the willing, waiting, eager attitude of a weak, struggling soul, in the presence of One who is able to save. When we thus feel our need, and thus venture our all on Christ, we learn by experience what prayer is, and sweetly know its answer too."—*Editor Michigan Christian Advocate.*

"Prayer makes the darkened cloud withdraw,
  Prayer climbs the ladder Jacob saw,
  Gives exercise to faith and love,
  Brings every blessing from above."

WHAT ACCEPTABLE PRAYER INCLUDES.

Acceptable prayer includes in it the offering up of the desires of the heart to God, agreeable to His will, and with a fervency of spirit proportioned to the blessing we ask for, in humble dependence on the Holy Spirit's help, a constant reference to the finished work and intercession of Christ, and a faith that is the "substance of things hoped for and the evidence of things not seen."

DISTINGUISH BETWEEN PRAYER AND FAITH.

I think we should understand the difference between prayer and faith; for there certainly is a difference. Though intimately associated in true prayer, yet one is not the other. Is faith prayer? No. Is prayer faith? No. Then they are distinct, though not independent of each other. It is true that there may be petition without saving faith, but there can be no saving faith without prayer, for prayer is the exercise of saving faith. There can be no true prayer without belief—natural or universal faith. Some measure of belief or natural faith must precede prayer. Yet prayer is the only way to saving faith. There can be no great development of faith, but by unceasing and importunate prayer. Prayer is knocking at the door; faith is the expectation

that it will be opened. Knocking is the voice of
expectation—of faith. Prayer is the breath that
fans the flame of faith, and when the flame of
faith reaches white heat it completely burns away
the dross of sin from the heart of the believer,
and the hands of sin and Satan that bind the poor
sinner, so that he has the power, and is free to
choose life. Thus faith and prayer blend, they
are reciprocal and interdependent. Hebrews 10:
22: "I will, therefore, that men pray everywhere,
lifting up holy hands without wrath or doubting." Here prayer co-ordinates with faith. It
stimulates the faith faculty. "Prayer is to faith
what the air and lungs are to the blood in our
physical system. The blood, pure and simple, is
the life, but the lungs receive the air, decompose,
transmute and appropriate it. In other words,
the air and lungs make the blood. So with prayer,
while it is not the condition of salvation, it con-
tributes to make that which is the condition."
Prayer arouses and puts faith to its work. To
call on God implies confidence in God, and confidence in action by prayer, is transmuted into the
human element, in saving faith. Faith is the
seraph, prayer wings it to Heaven.

EFFECTUAL PRAYER IS THE PRAYER OF FAITH.

Millions of prayers are offered, unaccompanied by faith. Listen to a thousand **prayers** (alas for the seeming necessity for saying this); listen to the current prayers that multitudes of Christian people put up at the family altar, in prayer-meetings and in the pulpit. Ponder those words, pointless, common-place circumlocutions, often prolonged; those wordy addresses and frigid formalities. Ah! Where is the faith? Such prayers are not only faithless, but purely human—nothing of the prayer of the Holy Ghost in them; hence they do not reach the ear of God. Prayer without faith is dead, being alone.

WHAT IS PREVAILING PRAYER?

Prevailing prayer is the prayer that infallibly secures the object asked for, and no other. "Whatsoever things ye desire when ye pray, believe that ye receive them, and ye shall have them" * * * the *identical* things asked, and believed for. "If a son shall ask bread of any of you that is a father, will he give him a stone? Or if he ask a fish, give him a serpent?" This subject should be looked at from, at least, three different points of view. (1) If there is a specific promise, or any other evidence, that God is willing to bestow the favor asked, and if the required faith is exercised, the identical favor

promised is granted. (2) But if there is no per-
ceived evidence that God is willing to answer our
prayer, we must pray with Christ: "If it be
possible, * * * nevertheless not my will but Thine
be done," i. e., "Father, if it is best to grant my
petition, Thy will be done; but if it is best not to
grant it, Thy will be done, not mine."

In this case, whether the answer be yes or no,
the prayer is answered, and the favor sought is
granted. Every true prayer, that has no per-
ceived evidence of God's will, says: "Father, if
it be Thy will (if best), to grant the favor asked,
then bestow it; but if it be not Thy will to bestow
the favor, then withhold it. I ask that Thy will
be done, not mine. If my desire can be granted,
I shall be grateful, but if not, I shall be equally
grateful."

Still again, suppose there is no known evidence of God's will, as to a favor asked in prayer;
and further, suppose it to be contrary to God's
will that the petition be granted, yet God may
answer, not the *petition* but the *petitioner*. An
illustration of this important distinction is found
in Paul's case, when he prayed for the removal
of the thorn. God did not grant his petition. He
did not remove the thorn, but he answered Paul,

when He said to him: "My grace is sufficient for you."

PREVAILING PRAYER GETS WHAT IT ASKS.

Dr. Wisner made the following statement to Dr. Patton: "I took one of my elders with me (where he was going to assist a brother in special meetings); that evening my elder led the devotions in family prayer, and poured out his soul in great fervency, for the conversion of sinners He earnestly besought the Lord, that He would ·so trouble the impenitent, that they would feel constrained to awaken us in the night to inquire what they should do to be saved; * * * about midnight the pastor came into our room and awoke us, to, tell us that a number of sinners had collected at the Academy, who were so distressed with their lost condition, that they had sent a request for us to visit them. * * * The next morning there were a number rejoicing in hope. * * * It was the Lord who answered that prayer, **by** giving us the *very thing prayed for."*

HOW MAY I OFFER PREVAILING PRAYER?

What an important question! How shall I answer it? How much may depend on the answer I give, God only knows. May be indirectly, the salvation or damnation of thousands of souls. "Lord, help *me*." How much may depend on how you hear and receive my answer. May be the salvation or damnation of thousands of souls. The Lord help *you*, my brethren.

(1) See, by searching your heart and life, and by a comparison of them with the requirements of God's Word, that you are in a state of heart, and so perfectly in accord with God, that you can claim God's promises as made to you, and put Him to their fulfillment. In other words, see that you are fully dedicated to God to do His will in everything, as He has revealed your duty in His Word. If this condition is not met, you need not inquire further. God will not hear your prayer.

(2) "Be filled with the Spirit." As He possesses you, He will illumine your mind, quicken your conscience, teach you what to pray for, and by His all-powerful intercession within you, enable you to offer the prayer of faith.

(3) Maintain uninterrupted "fellowship with the Father, and with his Son Jesus Christ."

(4) Obtain evidence from God's Word, His Spirit or Providence, that He is willing to bestow the blessing desired.

(5)   Having learned that God is willing (and He is, if your desire is legitimate) to answer favorably, cherish your desire until it is fanned into a flame. Become so profoundly, intensely, supremely interested in the object of your prayer, that everything else, at the time, must be entirely secondary, and if need be, laid aside— eating—sleeping—work—business, until God answers. How may I become so interested? Devoutly study the Word, to know your privilege and responsibility, and being "filled with the Spirit," who is infinitely solicitous that you should have an answer to your prayer, you will partake of His solicitude.

(6)   Lovingly, but with all your will power, resolve that in the name of Christ, by the help of the Holy Spirit, and with an eye to God's glory, you will have an answer to your prayer at any cost.

(7)   Claim the answer *at once*. You may have the answer at once, if you will *now* meet the conditions; and now, other things being equal, easier than at any other time. The longer you pray for anything, except in a living, appropriating faith, the harder it will be to prevail. Continue persistently, fervently, and if need be, vehemently, till God answers, "Yes, my trusting

child." Thus take the Word of God—the great
text book, and Christ as your Great Teacher; by
the helpful ministry of the Holy Spirit, study the
Word devoutly on this and kindred subjects, and
on your knees, *practice* what you learn. While
thus engaged, new lessons, new truths, new facts
from the Word, and directly from the mind of
the Spirit, who "shall lead you into all truth,"
will flash upon your mind. Thus study and practice, *study* and *practice,* every day, "in spirit and
in truth," and little by little each day, you will be
let into the wonderful and coveted secrets of access to, and power with God, in prayer.

There is no "royal road" up to the higher
altitudes of Christian attainment, where a single
human soul may conquer Heaven, earth and Hell.
Then be patient, but persistent. The great lessons of science and art have been learned by life-
long efforts, and shall we grow faint and give up
if we fail after a brief and half-hearted effort, to
wrest from the grip of the unknown, the most
precious lessons that God Himself can teach His
faithful child? While we may learn new and
more precious lessons in prayer every day, yet it
takes time; it takes a life-time to study this subject, for Christian science (real Christian
science) finds in the subject of prayer some of

the deepest problems—many of them unsolvable.
Nay, it will take eternity to fully understand this
subject.   Yet such are the joys of the eager
learner, and the blessings attendant on the exercise of an ever-increasing faith, that the greatest
encouragements are offered to *all*.   In this race
the victory is not to the rich, or great, but to the
humblest child of God.

BEST TIME TO LEARN HOW.

By far the best time to learn how to pray, is
in the *childhood* of Christian life, just as the best
time to lay the foundation for an education and
to begin to build thereon, is in childhood. Those
who neglect their education till they reach middle
life seldom become learned.   So those Christians
who fail during the first years of their Christian
lives, to learn how to pray—how to prevail in
prayer, seldom learn as easily as they might have
done and become as progressive students in the
school of prayer as they might have been, had
they from the beginning of their Christian lives,
been faithful in the study of the Word, and to
the promptings and leadings of the Holy Spirit,
who came into their hearts at conversion.   Every
young Christian should get into a *rut* as quickly
as possible, and *stay* there *as long as he lives*.   I
mean the rut of "praying without ceasing."   His

great business in this world is (1) to learn *how* to pray most effectually, and (2) to then *practice* what he has learned.

Definiteness in Prayer

The prayer that prevails is strikingly specific. It narrows itself right down to one object, which presses itself on the attention, and on the heart, and fills the vision, and becomes for the time the supreme object to be sought, and obtained, if need be, by the *supreme act* of the life of the petitioner. He who is cold and formal in his Christian life spreads his prayer out, and around the whole world, it may be, covering all subjects but the one most needed to be prayed for now, while the soul all alive and on fire, and in holy, intimate and conscious fellowship with "the Father, and with His Son Jesus Christ," focuses all the energies of his being, for the *present,* on just *one* object of prayer, and holds on for that till he gets it.

The End